# BLOCKCHAIN

*BLUEPRINT TO DISSECTING THE HIDDEN ECONOMY! - SMART CONTRACTS, BITCOIN AND FINANCIAL TECHNOLOGY*

BY: TONY SCOTT

© Copyright 2016 - All rights reserved.

In no way is it legal to reproduce, duplicate, or transmit any part of this document in either electronic means or in printed format. Recording of this publication is strictly prohibited and any storage of this document is not allowed unless with written permission from the publisher. All rights reserved.

The information provided herein is stated to be truthful and consistent, in that any liability, in terms of inattention or otherwise, by any usage or abuse of any policies, processes, or directions contained within is the solitary and utter responsibility of the recipient reader. Under no circumstances will any legal responsibility or blame be held against the publisher for any reparation, damages, or monetary loss due to the information herein, either directly or indirectly.

Respective authors own all copyrights not held by the publisher.

## Legal Notice:

This book is copyright protected. This is only for personal use. You cannot amend, distribute, sell, use, quote or paraphrase any part or the content within this book without the consent of the author or copyright owner. Legal action will be pursued if this is breached.

## Disclaimer Notice:

Please note the information contained within this document is for educational and entertainment purposes only. Every attempt has been made to provide accurate, up to date and reliable complete information. No warranties of any kind are expressed or implied. Readers acknowledge that the author is not engaging in the rendering of legal, financial, medical or professional advice.

By reading this document, the reader agrees that under no circumstances are we responsible for any losses, direct or indirect, which are incurred as a result of the use of information contained within this document, including, but not limited to, —errors, omissions, or inaccuracies.

# TABLE OF CONTENTS

Introduction .................................................................................... 7
Chapter One Blockchain: An Introduction ............................... 11
Chapter Two The History Of The Blockchain And Bitcoins ..... 19
Chapter Three Understanding The Technology And Features Of Blockchains .................................................................................. 27
Chapter Four The Pros And Cons Of Blockchain Technology .. 33
Chapter Five What Can Blockchains Enable? ........................... 41
Chapter Six The Incredible Impact That Blockchains Can Make On The Financial Industry ......................................................... 47
Chapter Seven The Potential Of Blockchains Lies Beyond The Financial Industry ...................................................................... 65
Chapter Eight An Introduction to Ethereum ............................. 89
Chapter Nine More Companies Interested In Leveraging Blockchains .............................................................................. 107
Chapter Ten The Ultimate Guide To Smart Contracts In Blockchain Technology ............................................................ 123
Chapter Eleven A Short Glossary of Important Terms Related To Blockchain Technology ............................................................ 133
Conclusion ................................................................................ 143

# INTRODUCTION

First of all, I thank you for purchasing this book. I hope that you find the information given here about blockchains to be useful.

What do you think of when you work with the internet? Of course, these days, the internet has become an inseparable part of our lives. Everyone seems to be using it and developing solutions with it. However, have you ever given thought to how radical this technology actually is? You see, things were widely different before the internet. There was a certain way business used to be conducted. When the internet was made available to the public, everything seemed to change overnight. Suddenly, business processes became much faster, and collaboration across distances was much easier. Of course, with further developments like chats and social networks, businesses had to adapt to the changes to remain viable. However, the change caused by the advent of the internet was drastic.

This is exactly what is going to happen with blockchain technology. As many modern businesses have experienced or know about the changes caused by the internet, they do understand the need for adapting quickly. This is exactly what they need to do with blockchain technology, and many of them have realized the enormous potential that it possesses.

So, what exactly can blockchain technology do? Well, there is a lot, and you will be learning all about it in this book. You will certainly be presented with the basic details and information you need to know about blockchains. More importantly, you will come to understand the massive potential and capabilities of the blockchain technology. We shall also be taking a look at the advantages that it can confer to any industry using it and the challenges blockchains need to overcome before it can truly realize the potential it has.

Of course, when we are talking about blockchains, we need to take a look at Bitcoin as well. After all, it was only due to Bitcoin that the world was presented with blockchain technology. We shall also be doing more than just learning about the technology. We are going to be looking into the effects that it can actually have in real life on the various industries. That is one of the most incredible things about this technology. The potential this technology has for disruption is not limited solely to the financial services industry but nearly all of them. Just think of any industry and blockchain technology has the potential to disrupt it even if the exact effects are still an unknown quantity.

We shall also be looking into the various companies that have started working with blockchain technology to provide solutions, products, and services. There is a considerable number of them. You will also get to learn about smart contracts which are one of the most important components of the blockchain technology. I have also included a glossary of the important terms at the end of this book so that it becomes easier for you to understand them. Simply head over to that section if you are stuck with a particular term.

So, what are you waiting for? Go ahead and enter the world of blockchain technology. Discover the incredibleness of this technology. Wishing you all the best in your journey!

## CHAPTER ONE

# BLOCKCHAIN: AN INTRODUCTION

Most people think of blockchains as the technology that has enabled the rise of the bitcoin digital currency. However, its potential exceeds much farther than that. In fact, it has become something more. These days, companies are coming face-to-face with several new challenges in the management and security of their data. Blockchain is developing a viable method for companies to verify as well as make transactions on a network immediately without the need for a central authority.

In fact, a significant number of major financial institutions among other organizations and industries are considering the use of blockchains to securely track the ownership of various assets. This can improve the speed of transactions while cutting costs and decreasing the risks of fraud. There are also firms that believe blockchains can help them monitor the movement of assets through the supply chains among other things.

In short, blockchain is turning out to be a massively important technology.

## What is a Blockchain?

A blockchain is a distributed database which maintains a list of records, each of which is known as blocks. This list keeps growing continuously, and the blockchain ensures that it is safe from revision and tampering. Each block will contain a timestamp along with a link to the previous block.

In the sphere of bitcoins, the blockchain is the public ledger of all the bitcoin transactions that have been executed. This ledger keeps growing as more blocks are added with the newer sets of recordings. Each block will be added to the existing blockchain in order that is linear as well as chronological.

Each node of the network will get a copy of this blockchain as soon as it joins the network. The copy gets downloaded automatically. The blockchain will also have complete details about the addresses along with their balances from the very first block, known as genesis block, to the most recent block that has been completed.

## Upgrading To Further Applications: Blockchain 2.0

While it was bitcoin that popularized the use of blockchains, the fact is that its range of potential applications is incredibly large. This technology enables the development of transactional applications which can establish trust and accountability while improving transparency. At the same time, it can streamline the business processes.

With it, the most basic business interactions can be upgraded for the digital world and thereby pave the way for new kinds of digital interactions. In fact, blockchains are capable of reducing the cost of cross-enterprise business procedures by a significant margin along with their complexity. The distributed ledger allows business networks to be created more easily and with a higher degree of cost-efficiency. It is possible to track and even trade almost anything without the need for any central control point.

The term Blockchain 2.0 was coined to denote the fact that this technology had moved on from being exclusive to bitcoins. This has become an emerging technology to watch out thanks to the promising applications across various business processes and industries.

## What Problems Can Blockchain Solve?

Currently, the methodology of assets ownership and their transfer between organizations is inefficient. It is also slow and expensive. More importantly, it has a high susceptibility to manipulation. After all, each organization will maintain their ledgers on their own. As such, discrepancies between the two parties can lead to increased settlement times.

The internet has certainly made a range of business processes easier and simpler. It has enabled companies to save a great deal of time. On the other hand, issues such as the ones mentioned above are still present because the underlying processes have not been upgraded to the digital age. As such, ways are required to prevent them from occurring in the future.

This is where blockchain technologies come to the fore. It can enable a ledger to be shared over the business network. This network will remain private among the parties concerned. A party will be able to join this network only after getting the requisite permission. Moreover, cryptographic technology will ensure the security of the network and enable the participants to view only what they have the authorization for.

The use of blockchain technology will improve the robustness of the shared ledger. After all, it will be distributed and replicated. All the transactions that go against the ledger will need consensus from the entire network to proceed. In the network, all the details and information will remain transparent. Additionally, transactions will be final and unchangeable.

With these features in place, it will be possible to provide the products and services in a more efficient manner. At the same time, it can become possible to lower the costs in various levels of service.

# The Key Concepts Related To Blockchain Technology

Due to the scope of blockchain technology, it is important to get familiar with the critical concepts that drive it. Only then will you be able to get a proper grasp of what the technology is about and what role it can play in the world.

There are two major concepts in a blockchain. The first is a business network. In this network, the members will be able to exchange items that have a value by means of a ledger. This ledger will be kept by the members, and its content will always remain synced with the other copies. There are a few other concepts to note. We shall be taking a look at each concept in turn now.

## A Business Network

This network will be featuring a peer-to-peer architecture that is decentralized. Its nodes will be the market participants like securities firms and banks. Of course, the network will be distributed. Protocol peers will be validating and committing transactions so as to reach a consensus.

## Shared Ledger

The ledger maintains all the details of the blockchain. As such, it is the source of truth for all the participants transacting on the blockchain. The ledger will record all the transactions taking place on the business network.

This ledger will be shared among all the participants by means of replication. As such, each participant will have their own copies of the ledger. However, it will be permission allowing participants to view only those transactions that they have access to.

**Smart Contracts**

Smart contracts contain digital assets which can be anything that has an owner and is capable of being converted into value. A digital asset can be either tangible or intangible. It is also possible for a smart contract to include a digital representation of sets of business rules.

A smart contract will be embedded into the blockchain and will be executed in a transaction. They will be verifiable and signed. They are encoded in programming languages.

**Consensus**

An entry in the ledger will be synchronized to all the ledgers of the network. Now, how do you ensure that all the shared ledgers are the exact copies of each other? This is done with the help of consensus. Consensus keeps all the ledgers synced together. As such, it can decrease the risk of fraudulent transactions taking place. After all, the tampering will need to take place across multiple places at the exact some time to successfully fraud a transaction.

For consensus to be achieved, all the parties will have to agree to the transaction and then validate it over the peer network. It is possible to establish rules for the validation of transactions. As a result, the participation is both trusted and trustless at the same time. It enables commitment to take place at a lowered cost.

**Confidentiality and Privacy**

It is quite possible to ensure these characteristics in the blockchain technology. You can protect the records with the help of a personal digital signature. The blockchain can generate a private as well as a public key for sealing the record.

The record will be encrypted and hashed. Once done, it will be sent to the network of nodes that have validated it. There will be unique IDs for the customer, reference and invoice numbers.

Now, the ledger will be shared in blockchain technology. However, it is possible for the participants to require certain things at times such as private transactions and identities which cannot be linked back to specific transactions. Such features can be implemented. Transactions will have to be authenticated, however. With the help of cryptography, these features can be implemented.

This is just the fundamentals of blockchains. The technology is rather expensive. As such, it merits a detailed look, from its origins to the possible roles it is going to play in the future. In the next chapter, we will be taking a look at the history of bitcoins.

CHAPTER TWO

# THE HISTORY OF THE BLOCKCHAIN AND BITCOINS

Now that you know a bit about blockchains let us take a look at how it came into being. Note that the history of blockchains is incredibly entwined with that of bitcoins. After all, blockchains came into being only due to the rise of bitcoins.

The blockchain came to be defined for the first time within the original source code for Bitcoin. It was developed as a solution to the then prevailing issue of getting a database to be secure without the need of a trusted administrator. Blockchain definitely succeeded in that matter. While the recent applications of blockchains seek to separate their use of the technology from its association with Bitcoin, that relationship still exists. As such, the history of bitcoins should also be understood before proceeding further.

## 2008

The roots of bitcoins stretch all the way back to 2008. An encryption patent application was submitted in August 2008. The application was filed by three individuals, Charles Bry, Vladimir Oksman and Neal Kin. They also register the domain bitcoin.org in the same month. All of them have denied having any connections with the alleged inventor of the bitcoin concept, Satoshi Nakamoto.

A few months later in October, the infamous white paper by Satoshi Nakamoto was released. In it, he revealed his idea for a completely P2P version of electronic cash. In his paper, he talked about he solved the issue of money being copied. As a result, it became a vital step in the legitimate growth of Bitcoin.

Satoshi Nakamoto is an alias and the real person behind Bitcoin has never been found despite several attempts to do so. Many of these attempts have received wide coverage, but nothing has come out of them.

## 2009

While the concept of Bitcoin was developed in 2008, it wasn't until 2009 that it actually came into being. In January, Satoshi launches the first block which comes to be known as Genesis. He begins to start mining Bitcoins. Also in January, the first transaction with bitcoins takes place when Satoshi sends a few to Hal Finney, a cryptographic activist, and a developer.

A few months later in October, bitcoin is recognized as a currency by getting an equivalent value in the traditional currencies. As per the New Liberty Standard, the value of bitcoin was established at 1,309 BTC for every 1 USD. The equation used to derive the value also takes into account the cost of electricity required to run the computers for mining bitcoins.

## 2010

By this time, bitcoin is really growing. In May, LasloHanyecz, a programmer in Florida, sent 10,000 BTC to a person in England. Around $25 worth of bitcoins was used for ordering a pizza for Hanyecz from Papa John's. That pizza is worth more than a million GBP by current estimations. As such, it is a major milestone in the history of bitcoins.

In August, Bitcoin experiences its first hack. A vulnerability was discovered in the process used by the system for the verification of the value of Bitcoin. As a result of this flaw, 184 billion bitcoins were generated. This causes the value of bitcoins to drop significantly.

The hack was just the first in a line of other vulnerabilities that were discovered in September. These flaws existed in the blockchain. Due to these issues, bitcoin began to get attention from governmental groups. A report is published on money laundering and how bitcoins can be a part of it. The report also suggests that bitcoin can end up helping people finance terrorist groups.

However, by November, bitcoin sees resurgence by reaching the $1 million mark.

## 2011

In February, bitcoin achieves parity with the US dollar for the very first time in its history.

## 2013

In March, the first regulation for bitcoins is issued by the US Financial Crimes Enforcement Network. This takes place as a guidance report for the people administering, using or exchanging virtual currency. This leads to a debate on how bitcoins can be regulated and this debate is yet to be satisfactorily resolved.

Bitcoin also witnesses its first major theft this year in June. The victim was all in vain, the founder of Bitcoin Forum. He stated that 25,000 BTC was stolen from his digital wallet. According to the conversion rates then, the equivalent value of the stolen bitcoins was $375,000 approximately. The major security breach in June also leads to the drop in Bitcoin value.

In August, Bitcoin is recognized as money when Federal Judge Mazzant states in a case that it can be used as money for purchasing services in goods and services. During this month, Bloomberg also starts experimenting with bitcoin data despite the presence of alternative tickets. The endorsement from a reputed organization like Bloomberg allows the bitcoin to enjoy more institutional legitimacy

Finally, in November, the US Senate starts the very first hearings on digital currency. This leads to a price hike of Bitcoin to $700. The then chairman of the Federal Reserve, Ben Bernanke, states that bitcoin may have long-term promise as long as the payment system becomes more efficient and more secure apart from being faster.

The central bank of China bans financial institutions in December from handling bitcoin transactions. This ban took place after the central bank stated that bitcoins do not enjoy the same legal status that fiat currency does. The ban also indicates that bitcoin is a threat to the financial stability and capital controls of China. Be that as it may, China is now the largest bitcoin trader in the world.

## 2014

In January, Elliptic, bitcoin custodians, launches the first insured storage service for bitcoins in the world for institutional clients.

A Fortune 100 insurer provides comprehensive insurance on the deposits which are held in full reserve.

Additionally, Overstock.com announces in January that it supports bitcoin payments in the US. Doing so makes it the first major online business of the world to accept Bitcoin.

In February, HMRC announces that bitcoin will be classified as private money or assets. As such, no VAT is going to be charged on the exchange or mining of bitcoin. As a result, bitcoin receives its most progressive treatment yet.

Later in this year, the US government shuts down Silk Road and auctions off over 29,000 bitcoins that were seized from it. Silk Road was an illegal online marketplace that used bitcoins for transactions. This helps bitcoin become more legitimate as the actions of the government show that criminals cannot use bitcoins to escape punishment. The bitcoin blockchain enables the identification of the users in most cases.

A major milestone in the history of bitcoin takes place in July 2014. The New York State Department of Financial Services publishes the first draft of its proposed rules for the regulation of bitcoins and other virtual currencies. Additionally, the European Banking Authority releases an analytical report that recommends EU legislators to consider the declaration of virtual currency exchanges as obliged entities. This will make the virtual currency exchanges start complying with the counter-terrorist and anti-money laundering financial requirements.

This report is quite vital as it allowed bitcoin to enter the financial mainstream. It showed that virtual currencies need a regulatory approach so as to achieve international coordination. That, in turn, will enable them to attain a regulatory regime that is successful.

In July, Bitcoin Investment Fund is launched by Global Advisors Bitcoin Investment Fund. This is the first regulated investment fund for bitcoins in the world. It enhances the legitimacy to bitcoin while giving way for regulated investors to start investing in it.

This concludes the short history lesson on bitcoins. As you can see, it has been a significant struggle for bitcoins to gain acceptance in the world of finance. Bitcoin has seen massive improvements since its humble beginnings. At the same time, the blockchain, at the heart of Bitcoin, has gone on and become more robust. It is easy to see why organizations that have seemingly nothing to do with bitcoins have noticed the blockchain and have started experimenting with it. After all, the rise of bitcoins has only been possible due to the blockchain.

CHAPTER THREE

# UNDERSTANDING THE TECHNOLOGY AND FEATURES OF BLOCKCHAINS

We did take a look at the definition and a few basics of blockchain in the first chapter. However, that is in no way enough to understand what this technology is. As such, we will be taking a look at the details in this chapter.

## The Distributed Database Feature

This is one of the most important features of blockchains. Since it is a distributed database, the database will exist in the form of multiple copies located across multiple computers. Those computers will together form a P2P or peer-to-peer network. As a result, there is no single central server of the database. Instead, the blockchain database will exist across a decentralized network. Each machine connected to the network will be a node in that network.

## The Use of Public Key Cryptography

It is the use of this kind of cryptography that ensures the security of the blockchain. On the blockchain, all the transactions will be signed digitally by means of public key cryptography.

Public key cryptography makes use of two keys. That increases the difficulty of cracking it. They are the public key and the private key. These keys are related mathematically. However, the math is incredibly complex. In fact, it is so complex that it is not computationally feasible to crack the math. In other words, it is almost impossible to guess the private key.

The public key is used for signing and encrypting the message that you are sending. The recipient will be able to use their private key to decrypt the message or transaction. The only private key that will work will be that of the designated recipient and nobody else's.

Apart from encrypting messages, it is possible to use public key cryptography to authenticate the identity. It can also provide verification that the message has not been changed in any way. This is especially important for the transactions on the blockchain.

## The Consensus

As you know, the blockchain database has a distributed nature. Due to this feature, the data about all the new transactions will have to be delivered to all the nodes of the network. This will ensure that the blockchain remains in sync as one single ledger instead of existing as multiple conflicting ledgers. Therefore, the distributed copies of the blockchain or ledger must be reconciled so as to contain the same data before the blockchain can be updated.

This occurs in the blockchain by means of a consensus process. In other words, the majority of the nodes of the network must be concurrent. It is this consensus process that is considered to be one of the most important features of the blockchain. The consensus process is emergent. There is no scheduled interval or time in which each new block and transaction are verified computationally.

## The Constituents of a Block

A blockchain is made up multiple blocks, and each of these blocks will have a list of transactions. Each of these blocks will also have a block header. The header is going to contain three sets of data at the very least. These three sets are given as follows

- Structured information on the transactions presents in the block.
- The data and the timestamp on the proof-of-work algorithm.

- The reference to the previous block by means of a hash.

The previous block is also known as the parent block while the hash is a cryptographic algorithm. It is the last set of data that creates the chain among the blocks in a blockchain. It is possible to use the hash of the header in order to identify a block in the blockchain.

## The Mining Process

The new blocks in a blockchain are created by the process known as mining. This process validates the new transactions and gets them added to the blockchain. In the case of Bitcoin, the time required mining a new block is 10 minutes. The machine which is mining is called the miner, and it will get financially rewarded when it mines a new block. As such, if it was mining in the bitcoin network, it will receive Bitcoin along with a percentage of the transaction fees for all of the transactions present on the block.

In the case of Bitcoin, for mining a new block, the miners present on the network will be competing to solve a math puzzle that is not only difficult but also unique. The proof of work of the solution will be included in the block header allowing the block to be verified. Solving the math puzzle is nontrivial.

Since the creation of Bitcoin, the difficulty of the puzzle has increased exponentially. This has increased the computational power required to solve it. According to estimates, Bitcoin miners are currently using more than 450 thousand trillion solutions every second to solve the puzzles. As such, it has necessitated the use of powerful computers dedicated to the task of mining exclusively. Some even pool their resources and create mining farms to maximize their returns.

These features certainly highlight the potential of blockchain technology. As such, it is specifically that organizations wish to exploit to improve their business processes in the future. Of course, the experimentation is still ongoing.

## CHAPTER FOUR

# THE PROS AND CONS OF BLOCKCHAIN TECHNOLOGY

Before we start using anything new, we do undertake a thorough examination of the item with respect to its advantages and disadvantages. Only when we find that the pros outweigh the cons do we go ahead and start using it. Why should blockchain technology be any different? You need to have a proper understanding of the benefits this technology is capable of offering along with the limitations or drawbacks it has. So, let us take a look at them.

**The Advantages of Blockchain Technology**

Of course, blockchain technology is advantageous. Otherwise, there would be no point for the various organizations to invest in their experiments with it. So, what are the advantages? Let us take a look at some of them.

**Trustless Exchange and Disintermediation**

Disintermediation is one of the major features of blockchains. It allows two parties to conduct an exchange without requiring the presence of a third party who can act as in intermediary or even oversee the exchange. This certainly speeds up the exchange. More importantly, it is capable of reducing the risks of counterparty. In fact, it might even eliminate counterparty entirely.

**The Empowerment of the Users**

This is something that is gaining traction in the world in various spheres of life these days. More and more people want to be in control of the information they share. This has led to innumerable debates on the dissemination of user information through the internet. In the case of blockchain technology, there are no such worries. It inherently allows the users to remain in control of all the information. They can exercise the same level of control over their transactions.

**The High Quality of Data**

In a blockchain, the data is always synchronized. This helps in ensuring that the data is always complete and consistent across all nodes. Apart from the accuracy of the data, the fact that it is always available on time is a major benefit. Additionally, the data is disseminated across all the nodes and updated. As such, its availability is another benefit of blockchain technology. After all, it is possible to get the latest data simply by accessing the network.

### Enhanced Level of Protection

It is the inherent features of blockchains that make them so beneficial to organizations. Consider the decentralized nature of the blockchain technology. The absence of a central location means that there is no single point of failure. As such, it is not possible for anyone to hack a single node to gain control of the network. This increases the resiliency of the overall network against malicious attacks. Blockchain technology does not only possess a high level of durability but also enhanced longevity. After all, the network will remain unaffected even if the data at one node gets corrupted.

### The Process Integrity

There is often a concern of integrity as to the execution of transactions via traditional methods. This is not an issue with blockchains as it will contain protocols in place. As such, the users can trust their transactions to be executed in the exact manner specified by the protocols. There is no need to find and get a trusted third party to oversee things.

**The Presence of Immutability and Transparency**

Transparency is vital in transactions just like the confidentiality of the users. In a public blockchain, all the changes made will be viewable publicly by all the parties involved, resulting in transparency. Transparency ensures that the users remain on top of all the transactions that are taking place allowing the building of trust. Immutability is another crucial benefit. Any transaction that takes place will be immutable which means that they cannot be changed or deleted in any way. This can prevent cases of fraud.

**Simplification of the Ecosystem**

There are certainly a number of issues involved in maintaining multiple ledgers. In those cases, there is a greater scope for confusions. Moreover, there is going to be more clutter to deal with when conducting reviews of searches. A single ledger gets rid of all of these complications. This is why blockchains are considered to be a better approach by many.

**The Speed of Transactions**

One of the greatest benefits of blockchain technology lies in its ability to speed up transactions. A transaction between organizations can take many days to be settled finally. First, the transaction will be reviewed and then cleared before ultimately being settled. There are also the working hours to consider as these activities will not be taking place outside of the designated hours. The blockchain technology can change all of this. It can reduce the times required for the transaction to be settled to just a few minutes. More importantly, the transaction can be processed 24/7.

**Decrease in Transaction Costs**

This is a significant benefit offered by blockchain technology and one of the major reasons why organizations are interested in it. In a blockchain, there is no need for any third parties and intermediaries. As such, any expenses related to them are instantly eliminated. Moreover, there are no overhead expenses related to the exchange of assets. These things enable blockchains to have the potential of greatly reducing the fees associated with each transaction.

## The Challenges of Blockchain Technology

It would not be completely correct to define the following as the disadvantages of this technology. After all, it is quite possible to develop solutions to overcome them. It might not be possible for those solutions to be available at the current moment. However, with time, solutions will be found. As such, they are challenges that need to be surmounted.

## The Infantile Technology

While blockchain technology certainly holds great promise, the fact is that it is still in its nascent stages. There are several challenges that need to be resolved first before it can properly and achieve its potential. Some issues that need to be worked out include data limits, the verification process, and transaction speed among others. Once these have been taken care of, the technology will certainly witness an increase in adoption.

## The Hazy Regulatory Status

Let's face it. Modern currencies have always been in the hands of the national government. It is the government who has created the currency and regulated it. Bitcoins and, by extension, blockchains go against this norm. As such, there is very little regulation around their use. While steps are being taken to improve this scenario, they are still far from perfect. It is also stopping financial instructions from making widespread use of this technology. Therefore, the regulation status needs to be settled by the governments as soon as possible.

## The High Energy Consumption

As you have seen previously, the miners in the bitcoin network are trying out more than 450 thousand trillion solutions every second in order to validate their transactions. This requires a substantial computing power. A typical home computer is incapable of handling the demands in the timeframe desired. As such, you need powerful computers, and these machines do consume a lot of power. At the same time, the computers need to work continuously without any downtime. This increases the energy requirements. Therefore, the energy consumption is too high to use this technology sustainably at the moment.

**The Lack of Control, Privacy and Security**

Blockchain technology does address issues of security and privacy through its inherent features. At the same time, there are solutions such as robust encryption which can help in improving the control and security by a great margin. However, they are far from perfect. As such, these security concerns have to be addressed. Without it, the general public is not going to entrust their data to this technology.

**The Concerns about Integration**

The fact is that blockchain is a rather radical technology. The solutions provided by it, while beneficial and incredible, can only be enjoyed if some major changes are made to the expositing systems. In some cases, it might even require the existing system to be replaced completely. As a result, the switch needs to be properly strategized by the companies before the transition can occur.

## The Issues with Adoption

In a blockchain, the network is completely decentralized, as you know. As such, the complete shift to such a network will only be possible with the buy-in of its operators and users. Unless they are all ready to make the shift, there will remain issues with the adoption.

## The Initial Costs

This is a major stumbling block for the adoption of blockchain technology. Blockchain is certainly capable of helping its users enjoy significant savings in terms of transaction fees and costs. It is also possible to save a considerable amount of time. On the other hand, the initial costs are rather high. Organizations seeking to make the transition will need to have a major capital to do so. As such, the financial outlay can act as a deterrent for most.

The blockchain technology is incredible. It does have some amazing benefits to offer. Unfortunately, it will be some time before those benefits are enjoyed. After all, the challenges need to be overcome, and the concerns addressed. Only then will this technology become truly beneficial.

# CHAPTER FIVE

# WHAT CAN BLOCKCHAINS ENABLE?

There is no denying that blockchain is an incredible technology.

We have already seen its features and its advantages. However, we have yet to see the impact that it is capable of making. Before we do so, we need to understand what can be enabled by the use of this technology. That is what we are going to be taking a look at in this chapter.

## The Creation of Digital Assets and Their Real-Time Movement

The blockchain is a lot like an exchange for assets. It is possible to use this technology to create digital assets. You can even manage those digital assets and get them transferred from one node to another. As you have seen, there is an absence of intermediaries to verify the viability of the transactions. This eliminates the delays caused by such verification processes. Additionally, you can keep track of the movement of those assets in real-time.

## Implementation of Trust Rules

In a blockchain, you can include the rules that are a representation of trust right inside the transactions. As a result, the blockchain becomes a method of validation for these transactions by means of the logic in the network. There is no need for a central authority or a database entry. As a result, the trust factor is created easily and becomes a part of the transaction directly.

## Proofs of Ownership

In the blockchain, documents can be stamped with the time. These documents can represent ownership or even rights. As a result, they can act as ironclad proofs that are also secured cryptographically. The availability of irrefutable proofs can enable a wide range of applications to be created with the help of the blockchain technology. We shall be seeing some of these applications later.

## Ownership of Identity and Representation

This is another interesting feature of blockchains. It is possible to get identities be they real, pseudonyms or anonymous to be uniquely mapped onto the blockchain. This enables you to be the owner of your own identity. You do not have to worry about having your identities being controlled by Facebook or Google.

## Resistance to Censorship or Failure

The blockchain is made up of several resources and computers, all of which are decentralized. This certainly prevents the rise of a single point of failure as you already know. This enhances the resiliency of the network by a significant margin. However, this decentralization also enables the resiliency of the network against censorship.

## Development of Crypto-Currency Markets

In the majority of blockchains, a tokenization mechanism is present which is linked to a crypto-currency. This currency can be traded in various exchange markets. Of course, the creation and development of a liquid marketplace are not a compulsory requirement. Nonetheless, it is often the result of a successful blockchain.

## Capability of Running Services That Are Decentralized

New value is created when services are being run on the blockchain. For example, a decentralized marketplace can be developed based on the P2P protocol. On the other than, there is going to be a wide range of other blockchain services that will be available as soon as the technology is implemented. In fact, a new segment of applications can be developed through the addition of friendlier UI to the underlying services.

## Execution and Enforcement of Business Logic on Its Own

As you know, verification will be taken care of by the blockchain while the trust factor is inherent to the transaction. As a result, the transaction is going to clear itself. At the same time, the clearing of the assets and their settlement will be merged together.

## Selective Privacy and Transparency

It is possible to achieve them with the help of cryptographic technologies. This can bring about an improved level of data security and privacy that is decentralized. At the same time, it will become possible to verify the transactions without causing all of their details to be revealed.

## Reengineering the Business Processes

One of the most important things that can be enabled by the use of blockchains is the re-engineering of the business processes. Although rather difficult, it is certainly possible. Adoption of blockchains requires mostly changes in the business process. This is going to be the case, especially for the larger companies. After all, the required changes will be quite complicated.

## The Roles of Intermediaries

Since there are no intermediaries, blockchains are completely changing the role that they are going to play in the coming days.

This is a lot like how the introduction of the internet forced intermediaries like newspapers and travel agents to rethink their role.

## Newer Flows of Value

Money is not the only thing that has value. The blockchain is capable of acting as the perfect platform for the exchange of digital value. In fact, blockchains can ensure that digital value moves not only fast but also efficiently. The process will be free and cheap at the same time. As a result, it can become the new network for value exchange.

## Newer Regulatory and Legal Frameworks

In order to make the best possible use of blockchains, the legal and the regulatory frameworks must be modified. The current frameworks act as barriers to the proper utilization and implementation of blockchains. As such, the rise of blockchains will enable the creation of newer regulatory and legal frameworks that are adaptive towards the growth of this technology.

## Services Can Be Bundled

The blockchain will enable different services to be bundled easily. Of course, the services that will be bundled will be those that can benefit from working together. Take capital markets trading for example. In it, financial instruments can be cleared and settled together.

Blockchains are certainly capable of affecting a wide range of industries and business processes just like the Internet did on its advent. The first area to be affected will certainly be financial services. However, there are other areas that can soon start getting affected such as healthcare, supply chains, energy market, world trade and smart things. We shall see more of the impact made by this new technology in the next chapter.

## CHAPTER SIX

# THE INCREDIBLE IMPACT THAT BLOCKCHAINS CAN MAKE ON THE FINANCIAL INDUSTRY

Many consider the blockchain to be the next most amazing innovation after the advent of the Internet. This technology enables everyone to conduct transactions while remaining anonymous and yet everything will be completely transparent. The entire process revolving around a transaction not only becomes easier but also cheaper.

Of course, you already know these things. The great thing about blockchain is that this technology can apply to nearly everything that involves transactions or exchanges. Of course, the first industry that is going to experience the impact of this technology is the financial industry. After all, the blockchain came about with the rise of Bitcoins, a crypto-currency.

## How Blockchains Can Disrupt the Financial Industry

Many people consider that the financial services industry is ready for being disrupted. Of course, it depends greatly on how it approaches the transformation. Consider the things that this industry does. It moves and stores money. It can lend the money or trade it. The industry can also account for the money or attest to it among other things. Blockchains are capable of challenging and disrupting all of those functions.

This disruption can start in two waves. The first wave is going to focus on deeply automating the existing processes. This will be followed by the development of new innovations that are based on the use and application of the feature of crypto-technology.

In simpler terms, blockchain is capable of making the existing processes more secure and transparent. It can improve their efficiency while decreasing the costs. This will be the first way the technology will possibly disrupt the financial services industry. This will be followed by the creation of new products. The amazing thing is that it is not possible to state with any reasonable degree of accuracy as to the products we can be seeing in future.

It is a lot like the development of the Internet. Those who worked on what would eventually become the Internet could never have guessed that it would become so incredible with so many amazing features. In the same way, experts believe that it is not possible to predict what the future can bring in the way of blockchain technology.

While the second phase remains an enigma, the fact is that the financial institutions have already started on the first phase. They have realized the advantages that this technology can offer them. More importantly, they are slowly but steadily realizing the challenges that they will be facing with it. What is surprising is that the industry is actually excited to bring about the disruption on its own.

## Why Is the Financial Industry Working Towards Its Own Disruption?

One of the greatest surprises to experts is how the financial industry is treating blockchain technology. It took only a few years for the industry to place its focus on the technology after its release. In spite of this high level of focus, the industry is yet to be disrupted in any way by the technology. There are quite a few reasons as to why this is the case.

### A Few Possible Reasons

It is certainly possible that the financial institutions have yet to realize the changes that will be taking place in their business model. Alternatively, they might still be considering that blockchains are simply a better database that they can use.

It is also possible they have seen and learned from the other industries. They may have noticed how certain technologies could and disrupt the industry. After all, many financial institutions have been responsible for funding the very organizations that brought about those disruptions with those technologies. As such, these institutions might have started focusing on blockchains simply to be ahead of the curve.

**The Lack of Upgrades**

There is also a rather pragmatic reason why these institutions might have started focusing on blockchains. The fact is that the majority of the business processes used by the industry are far overdue for upgrades. It is a fact that the fundamental elements of the value transfer process used currently have remained unchanged for more than 150 years.

Clearing houses and banks have not made any significant change to the way they facilitate transfers for such an incredible duration of time. As such, it needs to be upgraded to meet the needs of the 21st century. This will be made possible by the use of blockchain technology. After all, the distributed ledger feature of this technology can eliminate the need for a trusted intermediary.

## The Rise of Startups

This is another reason why financial institutions have started to focus on blockchain technology so early. There are several financial technology companies on the rise. They have been making significant inroads into what was previously the territory of well-established institutions such as banks. As a response, banks and other institutions had to launch ventures and labs to test out newer technologies and even invest in these startups.

## So, Why Is This Happening?

These reasons are greatly affecting established financial institutions. They have already started implementing things such as strategy teams or incubators so as to remain on top of emergent technologies like blockchains.

Wall Street is one of those acting rapidly to incorporate newer technologies. The fact is that most of the revenue generated in Wall Street is by acting as the intermediaries. Since blockchains are likely to get rid of this role, Wall Street can witness a fall in their profits fast. By reducing the times required in transfers or exchanges, blockchains can make several jobs and technologies redundant.

Moreover, it is likely that the number of small payments will rise in the future. This will certainly increase the economic activity taking place. While the volume will be higher, the fees will be lower. As such, institutions are trying to implement these new technologies so that they can maintain or even grow their share in what is going to be a less profitable business in future.

## What Will Be the Early Stages of Disruption?

The fact is that the disruption caused by blockchain technology is greatly dependent on how it is leveraged by the financial institutions. In turn, the use of blockchain technology is dependent on the specific area in which the institution is focused on. After all, some of them are involved in trading while others are into commercial banking. There are also institutions that focus on SME banking services while others have their own management arms.

In other words, there is no single potential use of blockchains that can satisfy the requirements of the entire industry. Instead, these institutions have to approach the question with care. They need to discover the opportunities which will allow them to reduce their costs without resulting in the creation of incremental risk. Then, they will have to find out the opportunities that will allow them to generate the revenue.

There are two recent examples that serve amply as an illustration of the possible early disruption that can occur. In these examples, the institutions are involved in improving their existing processes with the help of this technology.

NASDAQ is trying to develop a private blockchain network which can enable them to automate the process of managing the shares of private companies. This is currently quite an onerous process at the moment. Another example is Gift. That institution is trying to enhance the security of gift certificates and cards. Currently, gift cards are at high risk for fraudulent cases. As such, they are exploring how a private blockchain network can enable the certificates to become cheaper and more secure.

Another kind of opportunity that we discussed was the creation of a new revenue stream. Let us consider a credit card network as an example to illustrate this. The network can start using blockchain so as to make micropayments possible. These payments will generally be too small for the traditional processing methods because of the fixed costs associated with credit card payments. As such, a credit card network just found a new stream of revenue with the help of blockchains.

The fact remains that disruption is going to take place. After all, there will be some financial institutions that will not use the opportunities made possible by blockchain technology. There can also be others who will start using the technology too late. An example would be institutions that have strongly established streams. They can find it difficult to innovate. The current profits they derive might make them hesitant or even reluctant to start using blockchain technology. This will be common for those institutions that generate revenue by holding the deposits of their customers.

## The Starting Advantages That Can Be Enjoyed

Institutions which are able to withstand the disruption will find that they have gained an edge over their competition, especially over startups. There are a few reasons why this is the case.

First of all, all institutions will have to comply with the new regulations and get the appropriate licenses. This can easily end up causing a significant expenditure of a few million dollars. At the same time, there will be maintenance fees to consider, and that can be as much as a few hundred thousand dollars every year. As such, startups are going to require additional venture capital funding simply to start complying with the regulations. On the other hand, established institutions will have no such worries as they will have years of profits to fall back into.

Another advantage that the early adopters will enjoy is that they can make use of the trust placed on them by consumers. Take bitcoin for example. It was originally meant to be a way for transferring money without the presence of any intermediary. As such, it was known as a trustless currency. After all, there is no need to trust a third party. Even so, the level of trust placed on bitcoins by average consumers is lower than the trust they place on the US Dollar or other similar currencies.

Therefore, existing institutions will be able to create digital assets that are more likely to be used by the consumers. After all, the consumers already trust the institutions.

## What Are the Challenges That Financial Institutions Will Face?

Despite the benefits of the trust factor, the fact is that the institutions may not find its effects to last for a long time. The current environment of the Internet has enabled new tech companies to capture the consumer trust. They have even been able to cut into the share that previously financial institutions enjoyed. Surveys have shown that people place more trust on PayPal, Facebook, and Google than they do with financial institutions like banks or card networks.

In fact, it has been noticed that the trust on these new companies is increasing at a higher rate while the trust on banks has lessened. Therefore, it is not possible to state accurately if established financial institutions can actually beat the new entrants to the industry.

There is another challenge that institutions have to face, and that is their own industry. In order to start using blockchains for their benefit, the institutions need to be willing to work with each other. A widespread adoption of this technology across the industry will enable them to make the best possible use of blockchains. There is no benefit to be had if only one institution uses it.

## The Key Uses of Blockchains in the Financial Industry

Keeping in mind the various key concepts of the blockchain technology, it is quite possible to explore some of the possible use cases in the financial industry. Keep in mind that there are already a few financial institutions that are examining these cases.

**Asset Registries**

It is possible to create asset registries with the blockchain technology. Once created, they can be deployed for managing nearly any asset class, from automobiles to aircraft. These registries will be able to provide a complete trail of ownership, valuation, and maintenance. Being unalterable, this trail can be easily used for auditing purposes.

**Regulatory Reporting**

Blockchains maintain a transaction history that cannot be modified and is in the chronological record. Moreover, the history is delivered in an accessible and transparent form. Now, there are various regulatory processes which require documents to proceed through certain states before achieving any given state.

These state changes can be recorded easily in the blockchain. As a result, a conclusive demonstration of the complication with the processes can be provided without the need for any intermediary. It is possible to extend this future and include features like proof of control or proof of audit. In those cases, every new version of the document can be modified to have been changed as per a defined set of rules. The results of these processes can significantly decrease the cost of ensuring compliance with the regulation.

**International Funds Transfer**

Currently, the process of international payments, known as SWIFT, requires the help of intermediaries in the form of correspondent banks. Only with their help will the payments reach the desired physical location. The process is certainly slow, and the customer fees are rather expensive. Moreover, there are bank risks involved due to the poor banking standards in certain areas.

Blockchain allows these institutions to make use of a new approach. After all, there are no geographical borders or intermediaries in it. At the same time, the process is completely transparent. These issues have been the bane of cross-border payments for a long time. As such, blockchains can improve this process significantly with the added advantages of rapid turnaround times and reduced fees.

There is another vital reason for considering the use of blockchains in international payments. Currently, the systems used for processing these payments are centralized, making them a perfect target for cyber criminals. While the SWIFT system is distributed over multiple locations, it still requires centralized control nodes that are maintained by all the participant banks. An attack on any node can cause the entire network to be weakened resulting in a theft. Blockchain can decentralize the system and implement a trustless consensus methodology. Attackers can only compromise the system if they were to gain control of 51% of the nodes at the same time. That is almost impossible.

**Issuance and Settlement of Securities**

This is something that has already been worked into the existing system. The Securities and Exchange Commission has given permission for public securities to be issued through blockchain technology. Known as post-trade processing, it allows the complex security arrangement among the multiple parties to be agreed upon and then stored in the distributed ledger. This can certainly reduce the costs of administration. At the same time, it decreases the risks of reneging on the trade by a party.

**Insurance Contracts**

The smart contracts feature of blockchains is certainly impressive. It allows the technology to facilitate setting up the insurance contracts and managing them. As a result, data accuracy is achieved. Moreover, the technology ensures that the correct payment is processed. The accuracy in settlement of the brokerage, premiums, claims and commissions will also be ensured. All the parties to any contract will be having access to the same exposure data. This can resolve the data quality issues that exist. It will also help in leveraging better models for measuring aggregate exposures. It can help in capital allocation decisions as well.

## Banks Who Are Investing In Blockchain Technology

There are quite a few financial institutions that are actively investing and researching blockchain technology at the moment. Given below are some of those that have expressed their interest in this technology. We shall also take a look as to how they

### NASDAQ

This major stock exchange firm had initially revealed that they intended to use blockchains for enhancing their capabilities on the Private Market Platform which are a new initiative that they had launched. This platform is meant to help private companies undertake pre-IPO trading.

**Deutsche Bank**

It was mentioned by the company that they were exploring different use cases of this technology. They were interested in the areas such as payments as well as the settlement of fiat currencies. Other things they were interested in were regulatory reporting and improving the post-trade processing services among other things. Experiments on the use of blockchain technology in these areas are being conducted by them at their innovation labs.

**DBS Bank**

DBS Bank was the organizers of a blockchain hackathon held in Singapore. They were partnered by StartupbootcampFinTech and Coin Republic. The Coin Republic is a bitcoin-based company in Singapore.

**Euro Banking Association**

A report was released by them in 2015 about the implications of the various crypto-technologies. As per the report, it noted that the technologies could be used by banks to decrease the costs of auditing and governance. They also mentioned that the technologies could help banks in providing better products and reduce the time to market.

## Standard Chartered Bank

The chief innovation officer of this bank has stated that it is possible to use blockchains to decrease the costs while improving the transparency of the financial transactions at the same time.

## US Federal Reserve

It is believed that the Federal Reserve is working with IBM on the development of a new digital payment system. This system is linked to the blockchain technology.

## Goldman Sachs

This bank was a participant in the funding round of Circle Internet Financial Ltd, a bitcoin startup. Apart from being their lead investor in the $50M funding round, the bank has made extensive reports on blockchain and bitcoin their annual publications.

## BBVA Ventures

This financial institution is known to be an investor in Coinbase. They have also released a research report that states there interest in the blockchain technology.

## Santander

This institution has claimed that they have around 25 use cases for the blockchain technology. They also have a team for researching the various uses of this technology in banking.

### UBS

UBS is known to have a cryptocurrency lab located in London. They are conducting experiments in the use of blockchain technology in areas like trading, settlements, payments and smart bonds. The institution is planning to create an enterprise-wide product with the help of Clematis. They have also mentioned that they have approximately 25 cases for this technology in finance.

### Barclays Bank

They have two bitcoin labs located in London. These labs are open for entrepreneurs, businesses, and coders who are interested in blockchain technology and bitcoin. The bank has also partnered with Safello for the development of different banking services with this technology. They are running accelerators that provide enthusiasts and startups interested in blockchain with mentors along with a change to work with it on specific projects. One of the companies that have managed to emerge from this accelerator program is Every ledger. The bank has claimed that they have 45 experiments on hand that they wish to perform internally on the blockchain.

### ANZ Bank

They have started working with Ripple to examine the potential use cases of this technology.

**SocieteGenerale**

They have plans to hire employees with expertise on cryptocurrency, the blockchain, and Bitcoin.

**BNP Paribas**

They are conducting experiments with blockchain technology with the aim of improving the speed of transactions.

**Citibank**

The bank has built three different systems which make use of distributed technologies based on blockchains. They have even developed their own version of bitcoin known as City coin. This currency is being used internally so as to help them get a better understanding of the digital currency trading systems.

The financial industry is certainly gearing up for the entrance of blockchain technology. It remains to be seen how disruptive this technology can be even though it has a lot of potentials to do so. There are, after all, several hurdles that stand in the way of seamless integration. Standardization is one of them. It is important for blockchains to be thought of as platforms where applications and entire ecosystems can be built. It is only then that the key strengths of the technology can be leveraged.

Next, we shall see how blockchain technology has the potential to drastically change the world apart from the financial industry.

# CHAPTER SEVEN

# THE POTENTIAL OF BLOCKCHAINS LIES BEYOND THE FINANCIAL INDUSTRY

There is a wide range of technologies that are being claimed that they will completely change the face of business in the next few years. Previously, it was the Internet that brought about a revolution in the way business was conducted. Even social media has made a major impact. Now, people are saying that the social web, robotics, big data or artificial intelligence is going to revolutionize the world of business.

While these technologies certainly have the ability to transform business, their impact will be nowhere close to the effect that can be made by the blockchain technology.

While the technology is complex, the idea behind it is a simple one. Now, think about the features that you have learned about blockchains. The globally distributed database, the high level of security and strong sense of trust are the features that enable blockchains to be the very first native digital medium revolving around value in the world. The first native medium revolving around information was the Internet. You can now see how it completely changed the world. Blockchain technology has the same kind of potential. As such, it has important ramifications for businesses and corporations around the world.

## How Will Blockchains Affect the Other Industries?

Most of the discussions around this technology have focused on its potential to revolutionize the financial services industry. You have already seen that it can keep costs low and reduce the complexity level of financial transactions. It can improve the transparency of transactions as well as the regulation. In fact, you have already seen the impact it has started to make in this industry. Be that as it may, it is also a fact that the blockchain technology is capable of affecting the entire world in profound ways.

When the Internet first became accessible to the public, there were several experts who discussed the impact that it would make on the businesses. They theorized that it would decrease the internal as well as the external transaction costs of the companies. This included the costs of coordination, communication, and search. That is why it came as a surprise when it was realized that the internet made only a peripheral impact on the business architecture. While the transaction costs certainly decreased, the drop was lesser than what the experts had prophesied.

Now, the blockchain technology focuses on value. Experts believe that this innovation can lead the internet into entering into its second generation by focusing not only on information but also value. It is certainly possible for blockchains to help decrease various transaction costs by a significant margin.

Consider the following example. Blockchains can enable the creation of a globally searchable ledger that contains details of all the transactions. This can bring about a massive lowering of the costs of search. With the help of smart contracts, blockchains can cause the costs associated with contracting, enforcing those contracts and making the payments to take a plunge. Adding autonomous agents to the blockchains may enable coordinating and agency costs to be eliminated completely. It may even bring about the development of distributed enterprises that require little or even no management.

Blockchains can also help in upgrading networked business models as it can support a wide range of new applications. For example, it can enable the creation of native payment systems which can run without banks or credit card companies. The absence of intermediaries like this can allow the costs and the times associated with transactions to be reduced.

The technology can help create reputation systems that are built on economic and social capital. These systems can be controlled by individuals instead of intermediaries such as credit rating services and rating agencies. This can change the dynamic between the companies and consumers. As you know, trustless transactions will become feasible. The ramifications of such possibilities are simply staggering.

Take the music industry for example. In it, intermediaries tend to take almost all of the value while the artists are the last to get paid last. As such, it is ripe for disruption. This is exactly what a company named Mycelia is trying to do. Founded by Imogen Heap, a Grammy winner, this company has managed to develop intelligent songs that have smart contracts built in. This allows artists to sell their creations directly to the consumers without the need for a financial intermediary such as a label. As such, all licensing agreements and royalties are executed automatically and instantly. More importantly, the artists become the first to get paid.

That is just one of the possibilities of this technology. We are going to see more of these happening in the future.

## The Industries That Will Be Affected

Blockchain technology can disrupt a many great numbers of industries. Be that as it may, there will be a few that will be the first to face the brunt. The good thing is that there are already a few companies in those industries that have realized the impact that will be made by blockchains. As such, they have started developing processes and experiments to help them better utilize the technology. We shall be taking a look at each of these industries and companies in turn.

**The IP Industry**

When the internet first became a home for intellectual properties, many creators of these properties failed to receive their proper compensation. As such creators such as musicians, artists, photographers, journalists, designers and even scientists became beholden to various intermediaries. These intermediary agencies included film studios, record labels, galleries, publishers, universities and other corporations. Moreover, digital piracy became a commonplace occurrence which meant that the royalties due to these people were decreased.

The blockchain technology can be used as a new platform for these creators of intellectual properties so that they get the value out of their creativity. It can become a digital registry of the intellectual property with certificates of the condition, ownership, and authenticity.

One of the companies trying to implement this technology in solving IP issues is Ascribe. With the help of blockchains,

Ascribe allows artists to upload the digital art they have created on their own. The art can be watermarked as the original version and then transferred to the collection of the buyer. Of course, the version can move from the collection of one owner to the next in the same easy manner. It is a lot like how bitcoins operate.

As such, blockchains end up solving the double-spend problem in the intellectual property business in a much better manner than the current digital rights management systems. It gives artists the ability to decide where they want to deploy their intellectual property, when they want to do it and where.

**Sharing Economy Industry**

Blockchains are capable of creating a sharing economy that is much better than the one we have currently. At the moment, the majority of the companies in the sharing economy industry are more or less service aggregators actually.

These companies simply make use of the interest of the suppliers in selling their excess capabilities such as equipment and even handyman skills. They aggregate them via a centralized platform from which they resell to the consumers in need of the capabilities. During this process, the companies end up taking a portion of the profits and gather valuable data. This can be further exploited commercially by them.

The use of blockchain technology can allow the suppliers of these companies as a way to collaborate with each other. This allows them to enjoy a better share of the value generated.

Take Uber for example. Nearly everything provided by this ride-sharing service can be taken care of by smart agents on blockchains. The trust protocol in a blockchain will allow autonomous associations to be formed and then controlled by people who can come together for fulfilling common needs. The revenues from the services will be going to the members except for the overhead. The members will also be in control of the platform, and they will be the ones to make the decisions.

**Manufacturing Industry**

3D printing is most certainly one of the most remarkable of all the emerging technologies. It is shaping up to be another radical technology. It can bring manufacturers closer to the users and even make mass customization feasible.

Be that as it may, the makers still require centralized platforms from which they can sell their wares. They also have issues in protecting the intellectual property of their creations.

This technology will allow the rights and data holders to store metadata in nearly any substance such as aluminum or even human cells on the blockchain. This can end up removing much of the limitations of corporate manufacturing. At the same time, intellectual property will be protected. The availability of new open markets can also help sellers and buyers to contract in an easier manner.

The Internet of Things is certainly going to oversee trillions of daily transactions once it gets firmly entrenched. In order to manage such an incredible number of transactions on a daily basis, IoT will have to leverage the blockchain technology. After all, it will not be possible for the traditional financial services to manage these kinds of micropayments and settle the payments. In other words, you need a ledger that can manage everything when you are connecting the internet to everything.

**Enterprise Collaboration**

Currently, collaboration tools are bringing about changes in the nature of knowledge work and even management inside the organizations. However, the suites of tools that are currently being used have a few clear limitations. After all, central intermediaries are still required for the establishment of trust and also to coordinate much of the capabilities. As such, a system based on blockchain is certainly going to beneficial.

Consider the following example. It can enable employees to have their own distinct and elaborate profiles. Each employee will own their profile and be able to control it. As such, companies as well employees can keep their own data instead of giving it away to the larger social network companies.

There are a few development projects going on at MIT currently like Enigma. These projects demonstrate the usability of social networks created with blockchains. The networks, thus created, will feature a richer functionality with higher levels of customization. In them, data will remain protected, and the consumers will be better empowered as compared to the current networks. As such, the current companies need to embrace this technology to deliver better capabilities to the consumers or face disruption.

**Cybersecurity Industry**

The fact is that the ledger in a blockchain is public. Even so, all the data communications take place in a verified manner. They are sent with the help of advanced cryptographic techniques which ensures that the data has been sent by the correct sources. They also ensure that nothing has been intercepted during the delivery.

As such, widespread adoption of blockchain technology can certainly reduce the risks of hacking. After all, this technology is considered to be more robust than the majority of legacy systems. One of the ways this technology can reduce the current cybersecurity risks is by getting rid of nearly all the human intermediaries. The elimination of the need for intermediaries can decrease various potential security concerns such as corruption and hacking.

**Academic and Academic Records**

One of the more interesting uses of blockchain technology is in the field of academics. There is already an organization that is interested in exploring the potential uses of the technology in this field. The Albertson School is a software skills program based in California. It has announced its intention to make use of blockchain technologies for the authentication of academic certificates.

As a result, the students who claim that they have passed courses at this school will not be able to use accreditation that they did not earn. Now, imagine the possibilities when more schools start using this technology. It can give rise to transparency in transcripts, diplomas, and academic certificates. Therefore, it will become incredibly difficult to commit frauds of the kind mentioned above, and such frauds can be combatted in an easier manner. At the same time, it is possible to save a considerable amount of time and money by getting rid of manual checks and managing paper documents.

## Voting

Another interesting potential application of blockchain technology is in the area of voting. Consider what goes on for the sake of elections. For them, the identity of the voters must be authenticated. You will also have to keep records securely so as to track the votes. The tallies must be conducted in a trusted manner in order to determine who won the election.

Blockchains can be used as the medium on which the votes can be cast. This platform can also be used for tracking the votes and counting. As a result, voter fraud is something that can never happen. There will also be no issues caused by foul play or lost records. In this technology, the votes can be considered to be the transactions in the blockchain. An agreement can be reached on the final count by the voters as they can easily view and count the votes on their own. The inherent audit trail of the blockchain can help in verifying that the votes are not changed or removed in any way or illegitimate votes added.

One of the companies that are trying to bring together blockchain technology and voting is Follow My Vote. Their aim is to create an online voting system that is verifiable end to end.

## Automobile Sales and Leasing

The automobile industry is ripe for blockchain technology. Companies are slowly waking up to this fact. Take the partnership announced by DocuSign and Visa. They used blockchain for the creation of a proof of concept that can streamline the leasing process for cars. As per the concept, they developed; the entire process had just three steps. The consumer simply needs to click and then sign before they could drive off with the car.

In other words, the customer will choose the car they are interested in leasing and that transaction will be entered into the public ledger of the blockchain. The customer can then sign the lease agreement and the insurance policy. Interestingly, this can be done right from the driver's seat. Once done, the blockchain will get updated with that information.

However, it is quite possible for the technology to be improved upon further. With time, it might even be possible to implement this technology for car registration and car sales.

**Networking**

Quite a few companies are interested in using blockchain technology in networking. Samsung and IBM are among those companies. They have been working to develop a concept called ADEPT. Short for Autonomous Decentralized Peer-to-Peer Telemetry, this uses a technology similar to blockchains as the backbone for a network of IoT devices that is decentralized. In this technology, a blockchain will act as a public ledger for the huge number of devices. These devices will not need a central hub which can mediate the communication taking place between them. Since there is no central system for identifying or controlling the devices, the device can start communicating autonomously. They can take control of the management of bugs, software updates or even energy management.

There are quite a few other companies that are interested in using blockchains in an IoT platform. The filament is a company that is trying to use the blockchain to create a decentralized network for enabling the communication between sensors. This startup did manage to attract considerable attention during its funding stages.

**Forecasting**

Forecasting is a major industry, and blockchain technologies are capable of completely disrupting it. In fact, it is not just forecasting industries that will be affected. Industries are revolving around analysis, research and consulting will also be impacted.

Augur is one of those companies that are trying to do so. This online platform is currently being crowd funded. The company hopes to capitalize on prediction markets that are decentralized. Their service can seem like a traditional betting exchange at first. However, the entire process is going to be decentralized. Moreover, users of this platform can do more than just bet on stocks and sports. They can also bet on a wide variety of topics from natural disasters and elections. Their idea is to advance beyond gambling on sports and develop a predictions market.

**Online Music**

We have already taken a look as to how blockchain technology is going to affect the music industry. Let us now delve a little deeper and find out more about the potential applications of this technology in this industry.

There are quite a few music artists who are considering the use of blockchains to increase the fairness of sharing online music. There are also companies that are trying to do more such as increasing the volume of direct payments to the musicians. They are trying to use smart contracts for providing automatic solutions to licensing issues.

PeerTracks is one those companies. While it is still under development, the company wants to provide a music streaming platform which not only allows users to listen to the music but also make payments to the artists. It will be using blockchains to ensure that the users are paying the artists directly without the presence of any intermediaries. The platform also wants to increase the direct engagement between the consumers and the artists.

Ujo Music is another interested company. It has stated that it aims to rebuild the music industry with the blockchain technology. The company also hopes to find a solution to the issue of paying artists and streaming music. Apart from streaming, Ujo aims to become a much better catalog for songs, artists, and creators so that users can discover who exactly was behind a particular song. The company is going to use smart contracts to be the autonomous brains for the listings.

Of course, you have already read about Mycelia, formed by Imogen Heap.

**Ride Sharing**

Ride sharing services such as Uber are certainly anything but decentralized. After all, there is a single company which acts as the central hub for dispatching the services. The company uses its own algorithms to control the fleet of cars and also the amount that the drivers are charging.

This is going to be challenged by La'Zooz which is an Israeli startup. The company has expressed its aims of being an anti-Uber service. The company has developed a proprietary digital currency, similar to bitcoin. Blockchain technology is being used for recording the currency digitally. With it, people do not have to make use of a centralized network for calling cabs. Instead, they can use the service offered by La'Zooz to find other people who are traveling on the same route. In return for the ride, the users can exchange coins. The coins earned by the driver can be used for rides in the future. It is possible for the users to mine or earn the coins by allowing the app to track their locations.

**Real Estate Industry**

There are several issues with the real estate industry that are faced by consumers when they are purchasing or selling properties. First of all, there is a distinct lack of transparency during the transaction and even afterward. Of course, the amount of paperwork involved in the process is far too much. Errors are certainly a possibility, and they create additional issues and worries. Then there are lawsuits the risk of being defrauded. Shockingly, these are just some of the issues that plague the real estate industry.

By using blockchain technology, it is possible to decrease the need for keeping records on paper. It can also increase the speed with which transaction can be completed. Moreover, blockchain applications developed for the real estate industry can take over various processes such as recording, tracking and transferring the property deeds, land titles, and lines among other things. They will also make sure of the accuracy of the documents and make them easier to verify.

Ubiquity is one of the companies working to disrupt the real estate industry with blockchain technology. It provides a platform for mortgage companies and financial institutions among others. It aims to bring about security in the documents while increasing the transparency and decreasing the costs.

**Healthcare**

One of the biggest issues in the healthcare industry is that of security. Healthcare facilities are unable to share data in a secure manner across platforms. There are some very important reasons why this should be taken care of as soon as possible. By improving the collaboration among providers with their data, it becomes possible to increase the rates of accurate diagnoses. It can also enhance the probabilities of effective treatments. In short, it can increase the overall ability of the healthcare systems to deliver high-quality care in a cost-effective manner.

The use of blockchain technologies will allow the hospitals, patients, and other parties present in the value-chain of the healthcare industry to share the access to their networks easily. More importantly, it will do so without compromising the security and the integrity of the data.

Gem is a startup that is looking to into the use of this technology in the healthcare sector. It has launched a platform called Gem Health Network that uses blockchains. This platform makes use of multi-factor authentication and multi-signature technologies to create a universal data infrastructure that is completely secure. Another startup with the similar approach is Tyrion. It has created a platform for storing data and data verification for the healthcare industry. Both of these companies have become partners of Philips Healthcare.

**Supply Chain Management**

One of the most prominent features of blockchain technology is that it allows the transactions to be monitored in a secure and a transparent manner. This is the feature that makes its inclusion in supply chain management systems an obvious decision. After all, supply chains can be considered to be a sequence of transaction nodes which are linked to products move from one point to another.

Blockchains will allow the transactions to be documented in a decentralized record that is completely permanent. The transactions will be recorded as soon as the product changes hands in the supply chain, from the point of manufacture to the point of sale. This reduces any delays of time, prevents extra costs and avoids human errors.

Due to the obvious benefits that can be provided by blockchain to the supply chain management systems, there are several startups who are trying to enter this sector. One of them is Provenance. This company is creating a traceability system for products and materials. Fluent is another company, and it provides an alternative platform for those seeking to lead into global supply chains. There is also Skuchain which develops products based on blockchains. These products are meant for the supply chain finance market as well as the business to business companies.

**Cloud Storage**

Cloud storage is one of those technologies that have made a major impact on the IT industry among others. However, the companies that offer this service tend to secure the data of the customers on a centralized server. This is a major issue as it increases the network vulnerability and thereby there is a greater risk of attacks and hacks.

Due to the decentralized nature of blockchains, it is possible to improve the cloud storage solutions provided to consumers. After all, the storage itself will be decentralized which reduces the risks of attacks that can cripple the system and cause widespread loss of data.

A company in providing this kind of solution is Story. They are currently beta testing a cloud storage network that has been based on blockchains. Their idea is to improve the security of the information stored in the cloud while reducing the transaction costs involved in such storage.

**Energy Management**

This is another industry that has traditionally always been centralized and that too at a high level. As such, it is an industry that can benefit significantly with the implementation of blockchain technology.

Consider the situation in the US. There, you will have to take the help of a reputed power holding company if you want to transact in energy. In the UK, you will have to deal with the National Grid. Alternatively, you can choose to work with a reseller which makes its purchases from a major electricity company.

Due to the various issues surrounding such a state of affairs, there are quite a few startups trying to do something different. Take Transactive Grid for example. This is a joint venture between Consensys and LO3 Energy. Consensys is an Ethereum outfit that is based in Brooklyn. Transactive Grid is hoping to use Ethereum blockchain technology to allow consumers to conduct transactions in decentralized energy generation schemes. In other words, it effectively makes it possible to generate energy, buy it or sell it to their neighbors.

LO3 Energy has a few other similar projects such as the Brooklyn Microgrid. They also have Project Exergy which is a proof of concept for the harnessing of the excess heat that is produced by computers.

**Sports Management**

Currently, the only entities that could effectively invest in athletes were sports management corporations and agencies. In other words, this is something that individuals could not do in an effective manner. That is why blockchain technology can disrupt the industry greatly. This technology can decentralize the process of providing athletes with funding. This can be done by giving fans the ability to enjoy a financial stake in the future of sports starts.

So far, there have not been any significant inroads in using this technology for investing in athletes and getting returns. Nonetheless, there is an organization which is trying to make this happen. This is the Jetcoin Institute. They are promoting the use of cyber currency which can be used by the fans for investing in the athletes that they favor. Later, the fans will get the opportunity to get a portion of some of the future earnings of the athlete. Fans will also be presented with certain perks such as seat upgrades and access to VIP events. The cyber currency being used by them has been termed Jetcoins. So far, the company has run experiments on this approach by partnering with the Hellas Verona FC, a football team of Italy that currently plays in Serie B.

**Loyalty Programs and Gift Cards**

Blockchain technology has the ability to improve these programs by a significant margin. Retailers who offer customers loyalty programs and gift cards tend to run quite a few risks while doing so. Moreover, it can be quite expensive to run these programs. Blockchains can reduce the costs and enhance the security significantly.

After all, there are fewer intermediaries involved in dealing with the issuance of the cards and process the sales transactions. On the other hand, gift cards that use blockchain technology can be acquired and used in a significantly more efficient manner that is cost-effective as well. The blockchain also enables the programs to take advantage of its verification capabilities to improve their levels of fraud prevention. This reduces the costs further. At the same time, it prohibits and prevents illegitimate users from making use of stolen accounts and cards.

Gyft is a well-known online platform for sending, purchasing and redeeming gift cards. It is owned by First Data. Gift has partnered with Chain which is one of the leading providers of blockchain infrastructure solutions. The aim of this partnership to run gift cards for a wide number of small businesses and companies on the blockchain. This new program is known as Gyft Block.

**Government**

It may sound surprising, but blockchain technology can actually be beneficial for the government and the public in quite a few ways. One of the areas where it can do so is in the distribution of aid as well as welfare. Blockchain technology is capable of streamlining public governance. It can, of course, keep it secure as well. This is due to the inherent features of the technology that you are already familiar with.

While the potential of the blockchain technology in this sphere is yet to be explored fully, there are certainly companies who are readying themselves to be a part of the change. One of them is GovCoin Systems Limited. This is a financial technology that is headquartered in London. It is currently supporting the government of the United Kingdom in the distribution of benefits.

There is certainly a lot that blockchain technology can do. However, the exact extent of the disruption can be brought about by it cannot be predicted accurately at all. After all, the potentials of this technology are yet to be explored in depth. The industries and areas that can be affected by the technology mentioned above are just a few. There may be much more waiting to be discovered.

# CHAPTER EIGHT

# AN INTRODUCTION TO ETHEREUM

There have been several instances of companies and organizations trying to follow in the steps of bitcoins. Their aim is not to replicate the success of Bitcoin but to take the concept further and improve on what is one of the most remarkable applications of technology. One of the leading platforms in this sector is Ethereum.

**What is Ethereum?**

Ethereum can be said to be a computing platform. Unlike other platforms, this one is public and distributed. Of course, it is based on blockchains and features smart contract functionality. Ethereum provides the Ethereum Virtual Machine or EVM for short. This is a decentralized virtual machine which is capable of executing peer to peer contracts with the help of a cryptocurrency known as either.

The initial proposal for Ethereum was given by VitalikButerin in late 2013. Buterin is a cryptocurrency programmer and researcher. The funding for the development of this platform was sourced from an online crowd sale which took place during the months of July and August in 2014.

**How Did It Start?**

VitalikButerin had initially described what was going to be Ethereum in a white paper. At that moment in 2013, Buterin was a programmer who was involved with Bitcoin. His aim was to create applications that were decentralized. It was Buterin who put forward the argument to the core developers of bitcoin that the platform required a more robust and powerful scripting language for the development of applications. However, he failed to gain the agreement he needed to go ahead with the plan. As such, he then proposed the developed a new platform which would use a more general scripting language. He believes that it is possible for a number of applications to benefit from software similar to Bitcoin.

It was in 2014 that the initial development of the Ethereum software project took place. It was undertaken by Ethereum Switzerland GmbH, a Swiss company. This was followed by the establishment of the Ethereum Foundation which is a Swiss nonprofit organization.

As mentioned earlier, the funding for the development was provided through a crowded sale. The participants of this sale bought the value token of Ethereum known as ether with the help of bitcoin, the other digital currency.

When Ethereum was finally launched, it did receive significant praise for the technical innovations it had managed to bring. Even so, questions were raised by many out of the concerns about the scalability and the security of the platform.

**The Launch of Ethereum**

The launch of the live blockchain of Ethereum took place on the 30th of July, 2015. Frontier is the name given to the initial version of this platform. The consensus algorithm makes use of the proof of work principle. Be that as it may, this is not going to last. It is expected that the later version of this platform will end up replacing that algorithm with one that makes use of the proof of stake principle.

By May 2016, it was noticed that the market capitalization of ether, the cryptocurrency of Ethereum, had crossed the US$1 billion mark. It was also noted that ether was proving to be a significant challenge to Bitcoin in spite of the fact that it was still relatively new to the market. This was made possible by providing a number of services which are not possible when using Bitcoin.

## The Smart Contracts of Ethereum

In short, smart contracts can be defined to be applications that have a state kept in the blockchain. A smart contract is capable of facilitating, enforcing or verifying the performance or even the negotiation of a contract. In Ethereum, it is possible to implement smart contracts in a range of Turing complete scripting languages.

**Issues in Public Blockchain Contracts**

There is one significant issue that is related to the usage of smart contracts on public blockchains. That issue is about the bugs and security holes. These kinds of bugs remain visible to everyone, but it is not possible to fix them quickly.

The world realized this when The DAO was hacked on 17th June 2016. The attacked could not be stopped quickly or even reverse it. As a result, the problematic contract had to be fixed with a hard fork. This certainly created a lot of controversies but it did manage to end up the restoring the hack transaction on the blockchain of Ethereum.

Currently, research is going on how formal verification can be used for expressing and proving non-trivial properties. According to a report from Microsoft Research, writing a strong, smart contract is rather difficult in practice. The DAO hack was a perfect example of this situation. The report also went ahead to discuss the tools which had been developed by Microsoft for the verification of contracts. It noticed that analysis, on a large scale, of published contracts has a chance to expose vulnerabilities that have been widespread. It was also stated by the report that it is possible to check the equivalence of a program written in the language of Ethereum, Solidity, and the EVM code.

## What is Solidity?

Gavin Wood had defined a protocol in his Ethereum Yellow Paper and the Ethereum Virtual Machine currently works on this protocol which has been named Solidity. This programming language is a lot like JavaScript, and it was designed for the development of smart contracts which will be running on the Ethereum Virtual Machine.

Solidity can be compiled to bytecode, and that is executable on the Ethereum Virtual Machine. Solidity can be used by developers to write applications which can implement business logic that is self-enforcing and embodied in the smart contract. Systems have been developed by enterprise software vendors such as ConsenSys and Microsoft which are capable of translating commonly used programming languages into smart contracts coded with Solidity. For example, code written in Visual Basic can be translated easily into a smart contract written in Solidity with one of these systems.

## The Performance of Ethereum

One of the features of Ethereum is that all smart contracts get stored publicly on all of the nodes present in the blockchain. This can have a few problems in the long run. One of the downsides of this feature is that performance issues can occur. This is due to the fact that all of the nodes will be calculating all of the smart contracts in real time. This results in a significant drop in speed.

Engineers with Ethereum have been trying to share the calculations. Be that as it may, there have no solutions to this issue put forward so far. The Ethereum protocol is capable of processing 25 transactions every second as per the reports in January 2016. The actual speed might be different at the time of reading this book.

## The Uses and Applications

There have been quite a few proposed uses of the Ethereum platform related to smart contracts. After all, it is a lot like shared software which can use by everyone and yet remains safe from tampering. It is possible for higher-level software to use Ethereum in the establishment of online marketplace platforms.

Be that as it may, Ethereum is typically used as a platform for smart contracts, decentralized autonomous organizations and decentralized applications. By March 2016, Ethereum already had multiple applications built and functioning on it. The scope of these applications ranges across a wide variety of fields from finance to electricity pricing and even agriculture.

There are also many enterprise software companies who are currently testing the use of Ethereum in various applications related to their work. Some of the parties who have been known to be interested in such potential uses are IBM, JPMorgan Chase, and Microsoft.

Experiments are also being conducted to see if Ethereum can be used as a permission blockchain in a range of projects. Some have even started using it. JPMorgan Chase has already started the development of a blockchain on the top of Ethereum.

## Adoption of Ethereum and Related Issues

It was noted in March 2016 by the New York Times that the adoption of the Ethereum platform is still in its early stages. It also mentioned that there was a chance that Ethereum would end up encountering legal and technical issues in the future. These problems could slow down the growth of the platform. According to advocates of Bitcoin, it is possible for Ethereum to have more security issues compared to Bitcoin due to the increased complexity of its software.

One of the most notable adopters of Ethereum is Microsoft. The tech giant had announced that it was partnering with ConsenSys. This was a blockchain startup whose focus on the Ethereum technology. As a result of this partnership, customers of Microsoft Azure could enjoy access to third party tools which can enable them to experience blockchain applications based on the cloud and build with them. Some of the possible applications that can be experienced include cross-border payments and securities trading. Microsoft Azure is the cloud-based service provided by Microsoft.

## What Can You Do With Ethereum?

There is actually a lot that can be done with Ethereum. Consider the features of this platform first. The platform is decentralized which runs smart contracts. As a result, applications will run exactly in the way that they have been programmed. There is no possibility of any downtime or censorship. More importantly, fraud or even interference by third parties will not take place. As such, here are a few things that you can do with Ethereum.

### Develop Incredibly Powerful Applications

These applications will be running on a blockchain that has been custom built for them. They will be using a massively powerful and shared global infrastructure which is capable of moving value from one point to another while representing the ownership of property.

As a result of these features, developers are able to create enormous markets. They can store registries of promises or debts. Funds can also be moved in accordance with the instructions that have been given a long way in the past in a manner similar to a futures contract or a will. In fact, there are several more kinds of applications possible which are yet to be invented. Of course, all of this can be achieved without the presence of counterparty risk or requirement of any intermediary.

Consider traditional server architectures. In them, all applications will have to set up their own servers which can run their own code and that too in isolated silos. As a result, it becomes very difficult to share data. As a result, a majority of the users and other applications can get affected if even a single application goes offline or gets compromised.

This is not an issue with the blockchain. There, a node can be set up by anyone. This node can replicate all the requisite data for all of the nodes for reaching an agreement. The node can be compensated by the app developers and the users.

**The Presence of a Smart Wallet**

One of the interesting things about the Ethereum is the Ethereum Wallet. This can act as a gateway to a range of decentralized applications built on the Ethereumblokchain. With the wallet, you can hold or secure ether. At the same time, you can also handle a range of other crypto-assets that have been created on Ethereum. You also gain the ability to write smart contracts, deploy and use them as per your needs.

**Creation of Cryptocurrencies**

Another interesting usage of Ethereum is that you can create and issue a digital and tradable token. You can use this token as a currency or as a representation of some asset. The token can also act as a proof of membership or a virtual share among other things. The tokens will be using a standard coin API. As a result, your contract becomes automatically compatible with all wallets, exchanges or contracts that are using the Ethereum standard coin API.

Of course, you have the ability to set the total number of tokens in circulation to a fixed amount of your choosing. Alternatively, you can set it to fluctuate based on a ruleset that you have programmed.

**Starting a Project with Crowd Sales**

You may have ideas which you wish to develop with Ethereum? Of course, it is possible that you require help and funds in order to transform those ideas into reality. On the other hand, nobody will lend their own money to someone whom they do not trust.

This is where Ethereum can be beneficial. With it, a contract can be created which will store the money given by the contributor. The money will be held until a specific date or till a specific goal is reached. Based on the outcome, the money will be transferred to the requisite parties. In other words, the money will be released to you if the outcome was successful. If not, it will be returned back to the original contributors. The great thing is that all of this can be done without the need for any centralized arbitrator such as clearing house. Moreover, there is no need for anyone to trust anyone else.

If you have created a token, it can be put to good use here. The token can be used for tracking the distribution of the rewards.

**Creation of Democratic Autonomous Organization**

Once you have developed the idea and formed the organization, you will certainly require additional people helping you run it. You need managers to oversee the work and a trustworthy CFO for taking care of the accounts. Of course, board meetings will be necessary along with a huge amount of paperwork.

On the other hand, all of these things can be taken care of by an Ethereum contract. You can create contracts to collect the proposals from the people who provided the backing and contributions to your idea. You can also submit the proposals this way. All of this can be taken care of by means of a voting process that is completely transparent.

This is what is known as a democratic autonomous organization, and it has several advantages. One of these benefits is that your organization will remain immune to any influence from the outside or by third parties. After all, the contracts you made will only execute what was they were programmed for. This is ensured by the very nature of the contracts. Moreover, the decentralization of the Ethereum network is an added advantage. It makes sure that you can provide services that have a guarantee of uptime all of the time.

## The Potential Risks of Ethereum

Do not get blinded by the incredible benefits that are being offered by Ethereum. It is certainly an excellent and capable of the platform. Be that as it may, the fact is that the platform is still a young one. As such, it is prone to a range of risks that you should certainly know about. Some of those risks have been discussed as follows.

### The Youth

One of the best things about Ethereum is that so far it has been capable of taking more risks by adding new features. This is mainly because it has little to lose. You see, most of the history of Ethereum has taken place while it was worth only hundreds of millions of dollars. On the other hand, Bitcoin operates in the billions of dollars market segment.

As a result, as Ethereum keeps growing, it will begin to lose its ability to follow the principle of breaking things while moving fast. On the other hand, this is greatly dependent on the core development team. If they are of excellent quality, they can keep making progress and solidify their trust with the Ethereum community. If this is ensured, it is certainly possible for the execution to continue at this rapid pace.

**The Lack of Governance Crisis**

Ethereum is still quite young. As such, it is yet to experience a governance crisis. This has already been acknowledged by VitalikButerin. Unless a project hits a problem like a governance crisis, it is difficult to state if it is strong enough to last for a long time. As such, the tenacity of Ethereum needs to be tested, and it needs to be seen whether it has what it takes to succeed. Of course, it is more or less inevitable for successful projects to hit roadblocks as the vested interests of the people involved in it get bigger. Ethereum being a successful project, for now at the very least, is likely to experience such a crisis sooner or later.

**Heightened Regulatory Risk**

One of the advantages of Ethereum over Bitcoin is that it allows you to do more than what Bitcoin offers. On the other hand, this is also a problem as it increases the regulatory risks. Ethereum does not suffer a serious systemic risk because of this factor, however. Instead, it will be more of a risk to the specific applications of this platform. One of the possible examples is in the case of decentralized organizations. Those organizations are susceptible to regulations which are generally applied to a corporation.

**Increased Security Risk**

It may come as a surprise, but Ethereum does actually have an increased security risk. Even more surprising is the fact that the risk is due to the stronger programming language used by the platform. The robustness of the language results in a larger surface area where things can go wrong. Bitcoin has remained strong for more than 7 years and has overcome several issues. On the other hand, Ethereum is still young, and yet, it keeps more than $1 billion.

Apart from the DAO hack, there have not been any major issues on the platform yet. Be that as it may, there is certainly a likelihood of existing issues which people are not aware of yet. The chances of facing security risks increase with each passing day. People can end up creating smart contracts that contain bugs when using the Ethereum platform. However, it will not come out as a result of the core protocol in Ethereum.

**Proof of Stake**

There is a significant chance that Ethereum will try to move on to the proof of stake principle in the future. If it does work, then it will represent a major breakthrough in the technology. After all, it will get rid of the requirement of proof of work. It will also reduce the electricity and hardware requirements significantly. On the other hand, proof of stake also presents a major risk. Conducting extensive testing before the implementation may help in increasing the manageability of this risk.

**Scaling Issues**

Ethereum is susceptible to significant challenges with scaling. After all, it is difficult to scale the network when it is supporting mini-programs along with the basic processing of the transaction. This is a problem as there is no single solution that will work. Instead, a combination of solutions will be necessary. Of course, these solutions can end up being developed with time as the technology evolves.

Sharing the network can be one of the solutions for Ethereum. Moreover, the networks and the computing power are getting faster with time. Another probable solution is the economics of the blockchain in Ethereum only running the vital things as a forcing function.

There is another thing that can be done. This was put forward by Gavin Andresen. In this solution, the base transaction layer can be kept dumb for reasons of scaling while the advanced logic is placed in the higher layers. On the other hand, this process is not something that is being used in the creation of the interesting things at the moment. One reason for this is that it is more difficult to create. Another reason is that it is harder to ensure decent adoption of several layers in a stack as compared to having all of it right out of the box in Ethereum.

## The Relationship between Ethereum and Bitcoin: Love or Hate?

The fact is that it is difficult to state outright whether Ethereum and Bitcoin will end up competing with or complementing each other based on the current situation.

There is a chance that Bitcoin is the protocol which people are comfortable with when it comes to storing value. This is due to the reliability and stability of Bitcoin. As a result, Ethereum will have the opportunity to keep taking more risks by trying out advancements that have not yet been tested. In this case, Bitcoin will serve as a settlement network primarily. Ethereum will be used for running decentralized applications. As such, both of these can actually end up complementing each other.

However, there is a greater chance that Ethereum will end up overpowering Bitcoin and dominate it completely. After all, everything that Bitcoin is capable of can also be done by Ethereum. While Ethereum is yet to face and overcome major issues, the fact is that it is moving at a faster pace. Moreover, its leadership is better than that of Bitcoin, and it also enjoys a higher developer mindshare. Bitcoin may have the advantage of being the first. However, is quite possible that Ethereum will overtake it as per the current situation.

All of these things certainly bode well for the digital currency. Ethereum is taking the industry several strides forward and pushing the envelope of what is possible with the blockchain technology. The availability of competition and the presence of new ideas will enable better outcomes to be achieved. Ethereum has done a lot. Even if it ends up crashing and dying, the knowledge that the industry will have gained will be significant. As such, the industry is certainly going to thrive irrespective of what happens of Ethereum. At the same time, Ethereum is far from the only company experimenting with the potentials of blockchains. There are quite a few more. We shall be taking a look at some of them in the next chapter.

## CHAPTER NINE

# MORE COMPANIES INTERESTED IN LEVERAGING BLOCKCHAINS

It is easy to understand the interest of companies in blockchain technology. After all, it is one of the most incredible technologies of recent years if not the most remarkable. Due to the many potential uses of this technology, there has been the rise of several companies that are trying to leverage this technology for use in specific industries. You have already come across a few of them in the preceding chapters. Here, we will be taking a look at some more.

**HelloBlock**

This is a Bitcoin infrastructure that has been created specifically for developers. HelloBlock is the creation of Sidney Zhang. Zhang and his team have been responsible for the creation of a range of Bitcoin projects. After working on them, they found that the developer infrastructure to be primitive and raw. According to them, the level of the current ecosystem is similar to the TCP/IP level of networking. Additionally, they found the testing process to take up a lot of time and to be tedious.

The fact is that developers in general wish to explore the Bitcoin protocol. After all, it brings some entirely novel possibilities with money. This is why HelloBlock was created. Their API is capable of reducing all of these complexities and difficulties into a JSON interface. As a result, developers can keep their focus entirely on their idea instead of infrastructure. Of course, the API is only the first step for this blockchain startup.

**Kraken**

Kraken is a trading platform for digital assets that is fully compliant. However, it goes beyond the simple limit or market orders. After all, it allows up to 9 extra kinds of advanced order types. Their future plans include the possibility of margin trading as well, but only pre-approved margin trading will take place.

The company has established itself to be a FOREX platform but for digital currencies. They are currently based in San Francisco. The team is currently being managed by a group of talented developers and early adopters.

**BTCJam**

This is a P2P lending platform that is based in San Francisco. It managed to provide more than $5 million in loans based on bitcoins. The company was founded in 2013, and it is being led by Celso Pitta from Brazil. Pitta has considerable experience in the industry in building statistical models while working at Citi. He also has firsthand experience with loans. After all, he lived in a country known for its high-interest rates.

**BlockCypher**

BlockCypher can be considered to be one of the first companies to offer platform-as-a-service infrastructure in Bitcoin. The company has managed to rebuild the entire bitcoin platform from the fundamental level and then optimized it for cloud technology. As a result, it managed to expose web APIs and even callbacks that can be used by developers who can use them for building and scaling applications in a much easier manner.

The team behind the company is being led by Catherine Nicholson who brought in a completely innovative thinking process in what has more or less been a segment dominated by males. Catherine shares a long history with MatthieuRiou, her co-founder, in building platforms of a large-scale together. Their aim is to bring about growth in the developer ecosystem in Bitcoin. At the same time, they encourage more women to start participating in this industry.

**DigitalTangibleTrust**

The aim of this company is to be a provider of liquidity and a partner for marketing for hard assets. While these hard assets are hard to monetize, they can be digitized more easily into cryptocurrencies. Then, they can be traded on any exchange, peer to peer or centralized. In other words, they are trying to make it easier to purchase, say, digital mineral rights or digital gold bullion in another country or state.

The company is being led by a team in San Francisco. The team has considerable experience in marketing and crypto finance. They are working to push the envelope of innovation in blockchains by creating an investment portfolio which will contain coins. The coins will be issued by them as ownership rights to the unique assets. While the company was established in early 2014, it has managed to grow rapidly by having innumerable hard assets in their custody. They are interested in digitizing all things.

**Ripple Labs**

Based in San Francisco, Ripple Labs is a company that is creating infrastructure and commercial applications on the Ripple protocol. The company was established in 2012. It has managed to create a distributed exchange system that is crustless around a consensus ledger instead of a blockchain. The fact is that the two technologies share a lot of similarities. Additionally, some of the employees of the company have previously been developers for Bitcoin. Nonetheless, Ripple Labs is trying to bring the digital world to the traditional financial sector. By doing so, they hope to get the isolated payment systems under one single platform.

**Bifubao**

Known internationally as Bit for, this company is not an average wallet provider. This company is actually the first commercial developer who managed to implement a proof of reserves. The international team is based in Beijing, and it is made up of Chinese as well as American developers.

Proof of reserves is a technique that is based on Merkle tree, and it was developed in 2014 by Greg Maxell. It could allow hosted wallet companies and exchanges to offer cryptographic proof to members of the public that they possess the assets that they are claiming to have while preventing the exposure of the privacy of the customers.

**Coinbase**

The growth of this company has certainly been remarkable. It started off as a hosted wallet business in 2012. Currently, it is one of the biggest companies operating in the blockchain ecosystem. At the start in 2013, the then small company had only 13,000 wallets. By the end of 14 months, the number of wallets had crossed the 1 million mark. The company has also expanded its services. It now offers merchant support for other companies. One of their clients using this service is Overstock.com.

## BitPay

This is a payment gateway based in Atlanta, and it was one of the first payment systems that offered third party merchant support. The system used by this company allows merchants in accepting bitcoins. BitPay locks the bitcoins into fiat conversion rates so that the merchants can be protected from the fluctuations of the currency. After all, the value of Bitcoin tends to fluctuate significantly at times. The company now offers support to tens of thousands of companies.

## BitPagos

This company also operates in the merchant solution sector but with a difference. They do not just convert bitcoins into fiat currency. They are also working to help the merchants start moving in the other direction. In other words, they are trying to help the merchants accumulate bitcoins.

The company is being led by Sebastian Serrano. Being an Argentinian, he had experienced the rampant inflation that gripped the country in the early 2000s first hand. His company is based in San Francisco. However, the focus of BitPagos is the world at large, and they are especially interested in the emerging economies including those countries in Latin America.

## Provenance

The company is being led by Dr. Jutta Steiner and Jessi Baker both of whom are known for their incredible technological expertise. They have an in-depth understanding of not only cryptography but also supply chain engineering. As a result, they have a unique perspective on product proof of existence as well as transparency by means of the blockchain. Together they created Provenance which is a platform that provides data in real time. The platform can be used by brands to bring in a greater level of transparency by tracking the origins and the entire histories of the products. The technology used by this platform allows brands to gather stories and verify them easily. Moreover, they can be kept connected to the physical things and be embedded anywhere online.

Provenance is based in South East Asia. This area is host to a few important centers of financial services. However, the opportunity for disruption is greater in the commercial trade, logistics, and shipping sectors which are incredibly large in this area. In fact, out of the leading five shipping ports of the world, four of them can be found in this region. Underneath this massive industrial umbrella, there are an incredibly large number of industrial categories which can be served excellently by the platform offered by Provenance. One of the tasks that Provenance can help in is getting rid of counterfeit goods. It is quite possible for this platform to be beneficial for the art industry as well.

**Enigma**

This startup was formed out of the media lab at MIT. The company is being led by Guy Ziskind and Oz Nathan with Prof. Alex Pentland in an advisory role. Enigma is offering a decentralized cloud platform that ensures privacy. In fact, the private data is stored, analyzed and shared without being revealed in full to any party. The platform also allows multiparty computation to take place securely thanks to the use of the blockchain technology.

This is certainly one of the most radical uses of blockchain technology yet. It is quite futuristic as well. While this particular usage is still in the beta testing phase, the fact is that it is capable of being one of the most profound and exciting innovation with blockchain technology. After all, it ends up solving two of the most difficult issues in the technology sector in the current juncture, and they are security and privacy.

It is possible to layer this core function over the distributed cloud technology. The function is a dynamic combination which can transform how data is being kept and retrieved. It can allow a wide range of services in the civil, health and finance sectors to implement trust as well as security to their applications and upgrade them for the next generation.

## Consensys

Consensys can be said to be an antifragile organization. Led by Joseph Lubin, this company is built on the theoretical frameworks put forward by Ronald Coase. It follows a hub and spoke model which allows a loose collective of blockchain technologists to work on several verticals. Yet, the collective skills and understanding of these experts are leveraged together. There are quite a few companies who are working with Consensys such as Uport. You have also come across Ujo Music in this book previously, and that company works under the Consensys umbrella as well.

Currently, the company is trying to build upon the success they achieved with Block Apps. They are also collaborating with Microsoft on Azure. With the eventual growth of their core team, it is quite likely for this company to be the brains behind some of the most exciting innovations in the blockchain technology in the coming days.

## Encore

Ethcore is actually a small branch of the Ethereum Project. This is being led by Dr. Gavin Wood who is the core C developer of the Ethereum Project as well as its co-founder. One of the most remarkable things about this company is the team which consists of some of the most famous names in this sector. There are thought leaders and hardcore developers in the team such as VitalikButerin and Dr. Jutta Steiner.

The aim of this team is to help organizations and businesses to start making use of blockchain technology so that they can benefit from the many opportunities it offers. Ethcore is into the development of innovative software solutions for industries and enterprises that can unlock the value and potential of decentralized technology. In fact, the company is at the forefront of blockchain technology making it primed to be the driving force behind the changes in the industry for multinational corporations and even governments.

**IPFS**

IPFS is short for Interplanetary File System, and it tries to live up to their name which is most certainly a grand one. Their work can be said to be rewiring and even rerouting the entire internet. As a result, it will allow redundancy to be reduced by a significant margin so that everything can be accessed in the smoothest manner possible.

The company is headed by Juan Benet, one of the most prominent technologists and visionaries currently. IPFS provides a file system that is peer to peer distributed in nature. The aim of this platform is to connect all the computing devices with the same file systems. As such, it can be said to share some similarities to the Web but there is a crucial difference. IPFS can be considered to be one BitTorrent swarm which exchanges objects within a single Git repository. In simpler terms, IPFS will provide a block storage model that is content-addressed and has a high throughput. The model will also have content-addressed hyperlinks.

**Colony**

There are quite a few experts who consider Colony to be one of the most ambitious projects using the blockchain technology. It is quite thoughtful as well. It is being helmed by Jack Du Rose, a former artist, and designer. Before Colony, Jack was renowned as the jeweler responsible for the creation of the rather infamous Damien Hirst diamond skull.

With Colony, Jack wants to take on the future of work. To do so, they have created a decentralized autonomous organization that has been exceptionally designed. This organization replicates the structure of a company. However, there are no fallible individuals responsible for managing the company. Instead, Colony makes use of the wisdom and knowledge of the crowd through the application of artificial intelligence so as to ensure that the right things are being done by the correct people and that too at the right time. As a result, it becomes possible for people to come together for collaboration on projects of a large scale. In fact, they can even work on startups. At the same time, they will have a solid method for managing and measuring productivity. It will also provide the way for the people to get their payments. The colony has also made it possible for the creators to use a cryptocurrency created by the company known as nectar for the storage of value.

There have been several instances of companies taking notice of the creation of Colony. After all, the company has managed to solve a great deal of the issues that occur in an organization such as capital and talent localization. Even the difficult issue of providing compensation for an open source project has been tackled in an effective manner.

**SlockIt**

SlockIt operates in two areas of technology that are the most exciting at the current moment. These areas are blockchain technology and Internet of Things. The company is exploring how the light nodes of Ethereum that are embedded in connected homes, businesses and cars are capable of revolutionizing the Sharing Economy infrastructure that is on the rise. After all, it will allow any person to sell, rent or share their properties without the need for a middleman.

The company is being led by Stephan Tual who is one of the co-founders of the Ethereum project, along with two brothers, Simon Jentzch and ChristophJentzsch. The team of this company has been at the forefront of the intersection of these two massively important technologies for quite some time. They have managed to develop some rather interesting products revolving about mobility, connected devices, and even physical locks.

**Backfeed**

Backfeed has a team of highly skilled thought leaders and engineers. It is based in Tel Aviv. The company is into the development of resilient technology as well as new economic models that can support collaboration that is not only free but also systematic and spread over a large scale. The Backfeed protocols are based on the distributed governance model. These protocols have made it possible for the easy deployment and maintenance of decentralized organizations and applications which are reliant on the voluntary and spontaneous contribution of thousands or even millions of people.

Backfeed is being led by Dr. Matan Field who was a theoretical physicist before becoming an entrepreneur. He was also the one who founded LaZouz which was a decentralized and open source collaborative transportation system. As such, he is someone who is challenging the very notion of work and even organizations in this current age of globalization.

The company is building on the blockchain ecosystem to develop technology that is grassroots-powered. This technology should enable human cooperation to take place that is not affected by the scale of the project. The company provides tools which can ensure innovative economic models and resilient infrastructure. These, in turn, can promote the sustainability and viability of the decentralized communities apart from legacy organizations by means of equitable distribution of the co-created value.

To help you understand, take a look at the following example. Let's consider that the blockchain is like the TCP/IP of the internet. In that case, the platform and protocol being developed by Backfeed are like the web browser and HTTP protocol. Backfeed will make decentralized collaboration based on the blockchain as easy as it currently is to develop and deploy a new site at the moment.

**Plex**

While blockchain technology is capable of affecting the financial industry by a significant margin, the insurance sector of the industry is yet to receive any significant amount of attention from the enthusiasts of this technology. This is what makes Plex different. This company offers an automotive telematics platform. The platform makes use of artificial intelligence, machine learning and even Ethereum which is certainly something incredible. With their help, the platform will provide insurance companies with the diagnosis tics on the driver and the car remotely and, that too, in real time.

Automated driving can significantly impact the automobile segment of the insurance industry. The industry is also likely to be impacted by a range of other technologies. As such, exploring the potential applications of blockchain technology in this industry is an excellent idea. Plex is primed to take advantage of this idea already.

There are several other companies all trying to find out innovative ways to which blockchain technology can be applied to a specific industry. As such, some remarkable changes can happen in the coming few years. With the improvement of the base technology, it is certainly possible that the impact made by these companies will be incredible. It is not a question of if but rather of when.

## CHAPTER TEN

# THE ULTIMATE GUIDE TO SMART CONTRACTS IN BLOCKCHAIN TECHNOLOGY

Blockchain technology is not just about bitcoins as you have seen. One of the best things about the public cryptocurrencies is that it features robust security and that too at sustained levels. This has shown the world that blockchain technology is capable of providing incredible intangible benefits apart from improved efficiencies just like the internet did.

Be that as it may, blockchain technology is incredibly powerful as understandable from the examples given in the book in the preceding chapters. As such, they are capable of way more complex operations that are simply counting bitcoins come in. This is where smart contracts make their entry. In fact, they have already become one of the critical elements of enterprise applications on blockchain technology. It is already one of the mainstays of the technology.

Smart contracts will be a vital component for the next generation of platforms based on blockchain technology. Therefore, it is important to get a proper understanding of smart contracts, how they work and also how they are being used. While we have had a cursory glance into a smart contract in a previous chapter, we shall be delving in depth in this chapter.

**What is a Smart Contract?**

The smart contract is the term that is used for describing a computer program code which is capable of three things about the performance or the negotiation of an agreement. The agreement is the contract part of the smart contract, and three things the code does are given below.

- It facilitates the negotiation or the performance.

- It enforces the negotiation or the performance

- It executes the negotiation or the performance

All of these things are done with the help of blockchain technology. The entire process will be automated. As a result, a smart contract is capable of acting as a substitute or as a complement for legal contracts. In these cases, the terms of the smart contract will be recorded in a chosen computer language in the form of an instruction set. Smart contracts are also known as blockchain contracts, digital contracts or self-executing contracts.

## Understanding Smart Contracts

A smart contract can give a viable way for the issuance or the monitoring of the ownership of what is unique and digital representations of value. As such, smart contracts are fundamentally computer programs that are capable of acting as agreements. In them, the agreement terms can be programmed beforehand with the ability to execute and enforce on its own. The main aim of using smart contracts is to allow two anonymous parties to do business or trade with one another without the need for any intermediary or middle man. This typically takes over the internet.

One of the interesting things about smart contracts is that they are not the result of blockchain technology or even Bitcoins. Instead, their histories are much older, and their origins can be traced back to the 1990s. Smart contract as a term was first coined and used by Nick Szabo in 1993. Of course, Szabo is one of the alleged creators of bitcoin. The term was a reference to the computer programs which were self-automated and that could carry out the terms and conditions of any contract.

## Traditional Contracts vs. Smart Contracts

Experts believe that contracts will undergo a significant change in the future. They will follow a hybrid model that is made up of paper and code elements. In the future, contracts will be verified for their authenticity by means of the blockchain technology. However, paper backups will also be filed for the sake of traditional recourse.

Now, you need to understand exactly how smart contracts differ from traditional contracts.

**Traditional Contracts**

These are the physical contracts that are widely used these days. An example would be the contracts crafted by the legal professionals. They will make use of legal language, and they can be spread over a large number of printed documents. Additionally, they are heavily reliant on various third parties for their enforcement.

Of course, this kind of enforcement does end up consuming a lot of time. At the same time, the contracts suffer from a high degree of ambiguity. As such, there is a high chance for things to go astray. If this happens, the parties to the contract will typically have to refer to the public judicial system to find a remedy and resolution to the situation. This is an expensive process and can take up a lot of time.

**Smart Contracts**

Unlike traditional contracts, smart contracts are typically created by programmers by taking the help of development tools meant for writing smart contracts. As such, these contracts are digital in nature completely, and they make use of programming languages such as Java, Python, Go, and C++.

The code will define the rules of the contract as well as the consequences in the same way that a traditional contract does. As such, the smart contract will state the obligations, penalties and the benefits that will be due to each or either party in a range of circumstances. Once the code has been readied, it can be automatically executed by means of a distributed ledger system.

## How Do Smart Contracts Work?

If you wish to understand the workings of a smart contract, you have to first understand the difference between the code of the smart contract and how or what that specific code is applicable to. To help us better understand this, we can break down a smart contract into two distinct elements.

- Smart Contract Code: This is the code that gets stored, verified and then executed on the blockchain.

- Smart Legal Contracts: This is the use of the above code in the form of a substitute or as a complement for legal contracts.

## A Guide to the Workings of Smart Contracts

Here, you will find the general overview of how smart contracts tend to work on distributed ledgers. The steps have been given to make it easier to understand.

### The Coding

Here, the smart contract is created. The fact is that smart contracts work in the form of computer programs. As a result, it is vital that they function exactly in the way that the parties desire them to. This is made possible by the inclusion of proper logic as the smart contract is being written. The code will behave in ways have been defined previously. It will not possess the linguistic nuances that are a feature of human languages. That is why the code defines the part of traditional contracts that tell what action to be undertaken under specific circumstances.

### Distributed Ledgers

Here, the smart contract will be delivered to the requisite parties. Once the code has been written and checked, it will be encrypted. After encryption, it will be delivered to the other computers by means of a distributed network of ledgers. This can be done in one of two ways. A public permissionless blockchain can be used for sending the code. Bitcoin is an example of such a blockchain. In this case, the contract will be made in a way that is similar to how a network update of a transaction takes place. The another method for delivery is by means of a permission distributed ledger or a hybrid distributed blockchain,

## Execution

This is the step where the contracts are processed. Once all of the computers in the distributed ledgers network get the code, they will individually reach an agreement on the results of the execution of the code. The network will then get the distributed ledgers updated so that the execution of the smart contract is recorded. It will then start monitoring to ensure that the terms of the contract have been complied with.

In this kind of system, it is impossible for a single party to manipulate the execution process. After all, the execution of the smart contract will be in the hands of all the nodes in the network.

## A Potential Application of Smart Contract

To get a better understanding of how smart contracts can affect the various industries, it can help to consider a potential case. Here, we shall be taking a look at how smart contracts can affect the music industry. The fact is that it is possible to ensure a higher level of transparency to this industry with the help of smart contracts and blockchain technology.

Of course, there is an incredible range of practical uses cases in which blockchain technology can be applied to experience a lot of benefits. Smart contracts are certainly used in the majority of such applications. However, there is one industry in particular that can benefit a great deal with the help of smart contracts.

**The Current State of the Music Industry**

Currently, the music industry does suffer from a bit of complication. The rights of the music that have been created will be owned either by the musicians or by the record label. As the result of the ownership of the rights, the owner is entitled to receiving residual payments every single time that the music is made use of for commercial purposes.

The problem arises when someone wants to know who the actual owner of the music rights is. After all, it is vital to ensure that the payments are being directed to the right parties. Moreover, it also becomes difficult to calculate the exact share of the royalties that have to be given out as payments.

**How the Music Industry Can Benefit From the Use of Smart Contract**

For the music industry, the blockchain can be employed for tracking the ownership rights to the piece of music. It is possible to make the rights publically accessible to everyone. Now, you already know that a public blockchain database has an append-only nature. In other words, things can only be added to the database and nothing can be deleted. Therefore, the authenticity of the records will be ensured. After all, nobody can alter them.

Another potential benefit lies in the payments. The royalty payments can be transferred easily and in real time. Here, the smart contract will prove to be beneficial. It will be making sure that whenever a payment is generated for the specific work, the amount will be automatically divided into the terms that were set in the smart contract. As such, the account of each of the parties will instantly reflect that additional revenue has come in.

Smart contract is one of the important aspects of blockchain technology. It certainly possesses a considerable deal of potential. Knowing about it is vital if you wish to get a good understanding blockchain technology.

CHAPTER ELEVEN

# A SHORT GLOSSARY OF IMPORTANT TERMS RELATED TO BLOCKCHAIN TECHNOLOGY

Over the course of this book, you have come across a wide range of terms that are related to blockchain technology. Of course, remembering all of them can be difficult at first. This section should help by acting as a quick reference whenever you are stuck with a particular term.

**Address**

In blockchain technology, this refers to the cryptocurrency addresses. They are used for receiving and sending tractions on the network. The address will be a string consisting of alphanumeric characters. However, it can also be represented in the form of a QR code that can be scanned.

**Agreement Ledger**

This is a distributed ledger that can be used by two parties or more for the negotiation and finalization of the agreement.

**Attestation Ledger**

This is a distributed ledger that can provide a long-lasting record of commitments, agreements or statements. They can provide evidence or attestation that those commitments, statements or agreements had taken place.

**Bitcoin**

When used as 'Bitcoin' it refers to the popular cryptocurrency that has based on the proof of work technique application of blockchain. However, when it is used as 'bitcoin', it is a reference to the specific range of technologies that is used by the ledger of Bitcoin. It also refers to the currency as the currency itself is one of the technologies. After all, it provides the incentive to the miners to mine.

**Block Height**

This refers to the total number of blocks that have been connected to each other in the blockchain. Take Height 0 for example. It will be the very first block of the chain. This block is also known as the Genesis Block.

**Block Reward**

This is the reward which provided to a miner that has successfully managed to hash a transaction block. A block reward can be a mixture of transaction fees and coins. This depends on the policy that is applicable to that specific cryptocurrency. It also depends on whether all the coins have been mined successfully already.

**Central Ledger**

This refers to a ledger that is maintained and taken care of by a central agency.

**Confirmation**

Confirmation denotes that the given blockchain transaction has been checked and verified by the network. This is made possible by the process called mining if it is a proof of work system. After the confirmation of the transaction, it cannot be double spent or reversed. A transaction that has more confirmations will be harder to be compromised by a double spend attack.

**Consensus Process**

This is the process used by a group to reach consensus on the contents of the ledger. The group will be made up of peers who are responsible for the maintenance of the distributed ledger.

**Consensus Point**

This is the point where the peers will meet in order to agree on the state of the distributed ledger. This point can be defined in time. Alternatively, it can be stated in terms of a specific volume or number of records that have to be added to the given ledger.

**Cryptocurrency**

This is a type of digital currency that is based on mathematics. In it, encryption techniques are made use of for the regulation of the generation of the units of the currency. They will also be used for the verification of the transfer of funds. Moreover, cryptocurrencies will be operating independently of a centralized bank.

**Digital Commodity**

These commodities have specific features such as scarcity and intangibility. They can be transferred electronically and have a market value.

**Digital Identity**

This is a networked or an online identity that has been claimed or adopted in cyberspace by an entity. This entity can be an organization, an individual or even an electronic device.

**Distributed Ledger**

These are a kind of database which is spread over multiple sites, institutions or countries. Records will be stored sequentially in a ledger that is continuous. The data in a distributed ledger can be permission or uncommissioned which controls who will be able to see it.

**Double Spend**

This is a reference to a specific scenario in the network of Bitcoin. The scenario occurs when someone attempts to send a single transaction with bitcoins to two different recipients simultaneously. Of course, once one of those transactions get confirmed, it is almost impossible to spend it double. It becomes more difficult to double-spend bitcoins if that specific transaction has a higher number of confirmations.

**Genesis Block**

This is the absolute first block present in a blockchain.

**Hashrate**

This refers to the total number of hashes which can be performed by a miner within a specifically given period of time. Typically, the period is one second.

**Ledger**

This a record store that is append-only. Here, the records will be immutable, and they can contain more general information as compared to financial records.

**Mining**

This is the process by which transactions can be verified and then added to the blockchain. This process of finding a solution to cryptographic problems by the use of computing hardware can also cause cryptocurrencies to the released to the entity performing the mining.

**Multi-Signature**

Known as multi sig for short, it allows multiple parties to need multiple keys in order to authorize the transaction. The number of keys or signatures required will have been agreed upon at the creation of the address. A multi-signature address possesses a greater degree of resistance to theft.

**Off-Ledger Currency**

This is a currency that is minted off-ledger but is used on-ledger. If distributed ledgers are used for the management of national currency, then that currency is going to be considered to be off-ledger currency. It is one possible example.

## On-Ledger Currency

This is a currency that is minted and also used on on-ledger. Bitcoin as the cryptocurrency can be considered to be an example of such an on-ledger currency.

## Peer to Peer

Known as P2P for short, this is a reference to the decentralized interactions which can happen among two parties at the very least in a network that is highly interconnected. Participants in P2P will be dealing directly with one another through a single mediation point.

## Participant

This is any entity that is capable of accessing the ledger. They can read the records or add new records to the ledger.

## Peer

This is the entity that shares the responsibility for the maintenance of the identity and the integrity of the ledger.

## Permission Ledger

In this kind of ledger, the entities must possess the permission required for accessing the ledger. These ledgers may have a single or multiple owners. On the addition of a new record, the integrity of the ledger will be checked by means of a limited consensus process. The process will be carried out by the trusted entities. This makes the maintenance of a shared record a simpler process as compared to the consensus process that is made use of by uncommissioned ledgers. A permission block chain can provide datasets that are highly verifiable due to the digital signature created by the consensus process. This signature can be viewed by all of the parties. Additionally, a permission ledger will generally be faster as compared to an uncommissioned ledger.

**Private Key**

This is a string of data which can show you that you have access to the bitcoins present in a specific wallet. In other words, it is a lot like a password. Therefore, a private key must never be revealed to the entity. Only the person to whom it belongs should know it. Private keys allow the bitcoins to be spent from the wallet by means of a cryptographic signature.

**Proof of Stake**

This is an alternative system to proof of work. In this system, the existing stake of the entity in a cryptocurrency will be used for calculating the amount of that specific currency that can be mined by that entity.

**Proof of Work**

This is a system that links the mining capability of an entity to its computational power. In it, the blocks have to be hashed. While hashing is an easy process computationally speaking, an extra variable is added to this process to increase its difficulty. If a block is hashed successfully, the hashing is sure to have taken some time along with computational effort. As a result, a hashed block can be considered as proof of work.

**Smart Contracts**

These are contracts whose terms and conditions are recorded with computer programming language instead of the legal language. These contracts can be executed automatically by computing systems including an appropriately distributed ledger system.

**Tokenless Ledger**

These are distributed ledgers which do not need any native currency for its operation.

**Unpermissioned Ledger**

These ledgers do not have a single owner. In fact, it is not possible for them to be owned. Bitcoin is an example of this kind of ledger. They are used because they enable anyone to start contributing data to the ledger. Unpermissioned ledgers also allow everyone to have identical copies of the ledger. This results in an increased resistance against censorship. In other words, an entity cannot prevent the transaction from being added to the unpermissioned ledger. The integrity of the unpermissioned ledger is maintained by the participants by reaching consensus on the state of the ledger.

# CONCLUSION

With this, we have come to the end of the book. So, what have we learned? A considerable deal about blockchains certainly. Being one of the most pivotal technologies for our future, it was most surely a great idea to learn as much as possible about it. Let us recap for a bit.

We started by taking a look at what blockchains are. We then discovered how it came into being as a result of Bitcoin, another interesting thing that affected the world a great deal. Who knew that Bitcoin was more than just a virtual currency? We delved into the histories of this remarkable technology and got a glimpse of the amazing potential it has.

We looked into the several awesome features of blockchain technology such as distributed ledgers, security, and transparency. With the rising concerns about transparency and security in today's world, the capabilities of blockchain technology certainly seem remarkable.

Finally, we began to take a look at the capabilities of this technology in earnest. We discovered how disruption could occur due to blockchains and to what degree. As it turns out, this technology has the potential of disrupting nearly all kinds of industries. In fact, it may very well turn out to be as revolutionary as the Internet was once. We dived deeper and saw how each industry could be affected by the implementation of blockchain technology. Of course, the financial industry was our first stop. After all, blockchain technology came about due to bitcoins, which is a currency. That means that the financial industry is certainly susceptible to a great level of distribution.

Of course, we found that there were actually several institutions offering financial services that were already into this technology. They have already started experimenting with the technology and even formulated probable solutions to help them keep ahead of the curve. This is not limited to the financial industry as we saw later. There are several companies and startups that have started using blockchain technologies and are exploring its potential. Some of them have even started offering products and solutions. We took a look at Ethereum which is one of the platforms that is making use of blockchain technologies. In fact, it is only second to Bitcoin in terms of the value that it handles. So, it was certainly worth a visit. Then, we went ahead with smart contracts, one of the pivotal components of blockchain technology.

In short, we have gotten a very good idea about what blockchain technology is capable of.

I do hope that this book has been beneficial to you. So, where do you go from here? Well, you can start by increasing your knowledge about this technology further. There are several ways available online for the exploration of blockchains. With time, you may even be an expert in it.

Once again, I thank you for purchasing this book, and I wish you all the success in your life.

www.ingramcontent.com/pod-product-compliance
Lightning Source LLC
Chambersburg PA
CBHW071439180526
45170CB00001B/387